FINDING DUENDE

FINDING DUENDE

DUENDE: PLAY AND THEORY
IMAGINATION, INSPIRATION, EVASION

FEDERICO GARCÍA LORCA

Edited by José Javier León & Christopher Maurer
Translated by Christopher Maurer

Bilingual edition

SWAN ISLE PRESS

CHICAGO

Federico García Lorca (1898-1936) was one the most widely read and beloved poets and playwrights of twentieth-century Spain and one of the world's most influential modernist writers.

Christopher Maurer is professor of Spanish at Boston University and eminent translator of Federico García Lorca, Baltasar Gracián, and other prominent Spanish authors.

José Javier León teaches in the Center of Modern Languages, University of Granada, and is also author of numerous books and articles on Spanish literature and music including flamenco.

Swan Isle Press, Chicago 60611
© 2023 by Swan Isle Press
© Herederos de Federico García Lorca
Translation, Essays, & Notes© by Christopher Maurer
Essay & Notes© by José Javier León

First Edition
27 26 25 24 23   1 2 3 4 5
ISBN: 978-1-7361893-7-5

Swan Isle Press gratefully acknowledges Laura García Lorca, the heirs of Federico García Lorca, Fundación Federico García Lorca, and New Directions for respective permissions including, "Juego y teoría del duende" and "Imaginación, inspiración, evasión."

"Play and Theory of the Duende" by Federico Garcia Lorca, translated by Christopher Maurer, from IN SEARCH OF DUENDE, copyright ©1955,1998 by New Directions Publishing Corp. Copyright © Herederos de Federico Garcia Lorca. Translation © Christopher Maurer and Herederos de Federico Garcia Lorca. Reprinted by permission of New Directions Publishing Corp.

Library of Congress Cataloging-in-Publication Data
Names: García Lorca, Federico, 1898-1936, author. | León, José Javier, 1964- editor. | Maurer, Christopher, editor, translator. | García Lorca, Federico, 1898-1936. Juego y teoría del duende. | García Lorca, Federico, 1898-1936. Juego y teoría del duende. English. | García Lorca, Federico, 1898-1936. Imaginación, inspiración, evasión. | García Lorca, Federico, 1898-1936. Imaginación, inspiración, evasión. English.
Title: Finding duende : Duende, play and theory = Juego y teoría del duende ; Imagination, inspiration, evasion = Imaginación, inspiración, evasión / Federico García Lorca ; edited by José Javier León & Christopher Maurer ; translated by Christopher Maurer.
Description: Bilingual edition. | Chicago : Swan Isle Press, 2023. | Includes bibliographical references.
Identifiers: LCCN 2023036465 | ISBN 9781736189375 (trade paperback)
Subjects: LCSH: García Lorca, Federico, 1898-1936--Translations into English. | Creation (Literary, artistic, etc.) | Performing arts. | LCGFT: Lectures.
Classification: LCC PQ6613.A763 F56 2023 | DDC 868/.6209--dc23/eng/20230912
LC record available at https://lccn.loc.gov/2023036465

Swan Isle Press also gratefully acknowledges that this book has been made possible, in part, with the support and grants from the following:

BOSTON UNIVERSITY CENTER FOR THE HUMANITIES

LITERARY ARTS EMERGENCY FUND: ADMINISTERED BY THE AMERICAN ACADEMY OF AMERICAN POETS, COMMUNITY OF LITERARY MAGAZINES & PRESSES, NATIONAL BOOK FOUNDATION, SUPPORTED BY THE MELLON FOUNDATION

ILLINOIS ARTS COUNCIL AGENCY

EUROPE BAY GIVING TRUST

OTHER KIND DONORS

This paper meets the requirements of ANSI/NISO Z.39.48.-1992 (Permanence of Paper.

CONTENTS

FINDING DUENDE

FINDING DUENDE

1. Federico García Lorca speaking at the Teatro Avenida, Buenos Aires, where he read his lecture "Duende: Play and Theory" on November 14, 1933. The Avenida, he wrote, "is one of those huge American theaters, ten times bigger than the Teatro Español in Madrid." For the Argentine premiere of *Bodas de sangre* (Blood Wedding) "there were people standing in the hallways and hanging from the ceiling." Though popularly regarded as an "oral poet," García Lorca tried always to read from written remarks, rather than improvise. A few years earlier, he explained why to an audience in his birthplace, Fuente Vaqueros: "... I don't speak, I read. And if I don't speak it's because—the same as happens with Galdós and in general with all poets and writers—we are used to saying things quickly and exactly, and oratory seems a genre in which ideas become so diluted that all they leave is a pleasant music, and the rest is carried away on the wind" (*EC* 201).

FEDERICO GARCÍA LORCA'S LECTURE "DUENDE: PLAY AND THEORY" (1933)—the centerpiece of his poetics and a source of inspiration for modern artists and performers from Enrique Morente to Patti Smith, from Ridley Scott to Lawrence Ferlinghetti, Nick Cave or Amanda Gorman—has existed until now in editions and translations unfaithful enough to turn a lobster into a locust and transform the names of a Spanish prostitute and a family of butchers. No wonder. Lorca's duende–the dark, demonic creature who can intervene in the creation, performance and reception of a work of art—is a distant relation of the *duendes de la imprenta*, the imps who gather to do mischief in print shops, transforming, say, *cosa* into *rosa* or *sol* into *sal* (thing into rose, sun into salt.) With his professed distaste for the printed page—deathbed of poem, play or lecture—Lorca sometimes left it to his brother Francisco, his friends, and, after his death in August 1936, his editors, to tidy up: to compare copies and originals, punctuate, read proofs, worry over successive editions, and track down the manuscripts he had generously, sometimes impulsively given away to friends. Both lectures in this book were published posthumously. Lorca wrote "Juego y teoría del duende" on the *Conte Grande*, the Italian ocean liner taking him from Spain to Buenos Aires in October 1933, where he was to give a series of lectures and direct the performance of several of his plays. On his arrival he hired a secretary, and had him type out the lecture from his difficult handwriting. When the typist couldn't decipher a word, he guessed, or inserted a blank space which Lorca sometimes left that way, relying on memory of what he had written and not bothering to check his original.[1]

In 2018 the writer and flamenco scholar José Javier León collated manuscripts and typescripts and produced a critical edition that corrected those misreadings and lacunae. In a companion volume he modified decades of critical—and uncritical—thought about the lecture, and brought a smile to the lips of Lorca's readers:[2] far from home, on a stage in Buenos Aires, the poet had presented his own singular duende as an authentically Spanish tradition. With tongue in cheek, he served up the notion of an artist *having duende* as a popular expression in southern Spain, a slice of Andalusian folklore: "All over Andalusia—rock of Jaén or whorled shell of Cádiz—people speak constantly of the duende, and identify it accurately and instinctively wherever it appears," he wrote in 1933, adding that throughout Spain, and even in Argentina, people say, "That really has duende." Until now his readers have believed him.[3]

What José Javier León argues is that, although the word duende itself can be traced back centuries, the notion of an artist *having* duende— having a certain dark, mysterious charm that "everyone can feel but no philosopher explains"—was Lorca's own brilliant and playful creation; that, while Spaniards today might say that a performer *has* duende, they did so infrequently before Lorca popularized the expression; and that, although Andalusian guitarists and flamenco artists could refer to *duendes*, meaning musical ornaments or melismatic fioriture, the expression "tener duende" was seldom heard—or read—before Lorca climbed to the stage of the Teatro Avenida in October 1933 and enacted what he called "a simple lesson in the hidden, aching spirit of Spain."[4]

"Juego y teoría del duende"—a lecture which, by all accounts, mesmerized Lorca's audiences—first came to the attention of American readers, poets and performers in 1955, as an appendix to Ben Belitt's rewriting of Lorca's *Poet in New York*. Quickly embraced by American poets, it was explained at length to English-language readers by Edward Hirsch in *The Demon and the Angel* in 2002. By then the idea of duende, as found in Lorca, had become what Jonathan Mayhew calls a meme. Lorca's version of duende, associated principally with the bullfight and with flamenco, is now everywhere—applied to all the arts and trades, gracing shop signs and cookbooks, travel guides and the writing of an American poet laureate. It has been compared—dizzyingly—to Hebrew *dabar*, Plato's *enthousiasmós*, Nietzsche's Dionysos, and the *mojo* of Muddy Waters. Colm Tóibín called it "a heightened soulfulness," and—eluding false equivalencies like *star power, inspiration, charm, magnetism, trance or buzz*—the duende now haunts a *Dictionary of Untranslatables*. Though the word duende, as used by Lorca, has no English translation, duende has some easily identifiable qualities: it is an antagonistic, deathly, telluric, demonic, and irrational force—which Lorca often personifies—that can intervene at any moment in the creation, performance and reception of the arts. One of Lorca's most acute readers suggests that we think of duende not as thing but as *event*: an event so elusive that "Lorca himself did not strictly speaking represent it in a text but, rather, suggested its effects" (Quance 182). In his lecture, Lorca writes that the magical property of a poem is to "baptize in dark water" all who look at it—in other words, to thwart explanation, to remain mysterious. He did so in "Duende: Play and Theory," while defending his own poetics and the peculiarities of Spanish art.

Far less known than "Duende: Play and Theory," is an earlier lecture, "Imagination, Inspiration, Evasion," written at a crucial moment—one of emotional and aesthetic rupture—in Lorca's development as a poet. A fierce critique of his book of poems, *Primer romancero gitano* (*The Gypsy Ballads*), in the form of a letter from his intellectual fencing partner, Salvador Dalí, seems to have sparked Lorca to re-examine his belief in the central role of metaphor in poetry. What Dalí appears to have taught him—in that letter, in his painting, his essays and even in his own attempts at poetry—is that there is a better way of awakening poetic emotion than by lashing two distant objects together and revealing what they have in common. Metaphor resolves through analogy—through logic—the tension between sameness and difference. Symbolism, too, had a way of limiting the meaning of objects: for Dalí (as Lorca points out in his 1926 "Ode" to the painter) the flag, for example, was a simple joke. Dalí's advice to Lorca and to himself, in 1927-1928, could be reduced to a slogan: "Let things be themselves!"

> We must leave things free of the conventional ideas to which intelligence has subjugated them. At that moment those lovely little things will begin to act in accordance with their real, *consubstantial* manner of being. Let the things themselves decide where their shadows fall! And perhaps what we thought would cast a dense shadow will cast none at all, etc. etc. (*Sebastian's Arrows* 103)

What Dalí was calling for—his particular "evasion" of conventional poetry and conventional reality—was an energetic, voluntary sort of agnosia, a defamiliarization and non-recognition of everyday objects, stripped of their usual context, functions, associations, and symbolism.

When, in the *Gypsy Ballads*, Lorca mentions people riding horses, Dalí protests:

> [T]his is already too much, for in reality it would be better for you to ask whether it is really the rider who is on the horse; if the reins aren't really an organic extension of his very hands; if, in reality, the little hairs on the rider's balls aren't much faster than the horse; and if the horse isn't something immobile, fastened to the earth by vigorous roots.

Or take the minute-hands of a clock:

> The minute-hands of a clock (never mind my examples, I'm not exactly looking for poetic ones) begin to have real value at the moment they stop pointing out the hours and, losing their circular rhythm and the arbitrary role our intelligence has subjected them to (pointing out the hours), they evade the clock entirely and occupy the place that would correspond to the sex organs of bread crumbs. (*SA* 102)

The blowing up of "accepted" and "arbitrary" notions about things, each of these little explosions, produced images that Dalí—and Lorca after him—would call *hechos poéticos*: "poetic facts", or "poetic events."[5] Dalí's paintings or poems from 1927-1928 are an inventory of his own *fets poetics*: flying breasts, fingers, penises or eyeballs, rotten donkeys, queer apparatuses, headless torsos, a huge frozen toe, a puff of smoke, a grape pursuing an olive... Dalí was moving toward the Surrealism of *Le chien andalou*, and Lorca, who never subscribed to that movement, toward his own particular tension between the rational (the traditional metaphor) and the irrational (the image that defies or challenges logical explanation) in texts like his prose poems, his "Ode to the Most Holy Sacrament of the Altar," his drawings, his homoerotic drama *El público* (The Audience) and his masterpiece *Poet in New York*, which Lorca thought to be "full of what I call 'poetic events' [*hechos poéticos*] that answer to a purely poetic logic and the constructs of emotion and of poetic architecture" (*Poet in New York* 182).[6]

First delivered in October 1928, and repeated in Bilbao, New York and Havana in 1929-1930, "Imagination, Inspiration, Evasion" offers a binary (imagination vs. inspiration) view of poetic creation. As Andrew Anderson and others have noted, the 1928-30 lecture pays little attention to the third element in its title, evasion, which is seen as the outcome of "inspired" poetry, a cautious embrace of the irrational, a flight from what Dalí had called "the conventional ideas to which intelligence has subjugated things." Lorca barely mentions evasion in the lecture, leaving open the path toward duende, the enlivening yet deathly sort of inspiration, described a few years later, that will become his ultimate agent of evasion. The subtitles Lorca gave his lecture between 1928 and 1930 reveal the poet's uncertainty about whether those three elements—"Imagination, Inspiration, Evasion"—describe the "Mechanics of Poetry" (the three phases of the successful creative process), "Three Modes of Poetry" (pertaining to three types of poets?), or a recurring pattern, an eternal return, in "the grinding wheel of literary history." One thing *does* seem clear: Lorca describes his own past and future as a poet and, in the words of his brother Francisco (113), "brilliantly explains the functioning of his own creative mechanism."

Over the space of five years, from October 1928 to October 1933, from one lecture to the other, Lorca's written poetics will widen to include not only modes for creating poetry but also ways to create, perform, and receive poetry and music (from Bach to flamenco), painting, dance, and other forms of art and ritual, including the bullfight.[7] The 1933 lecture makes it clear that the duende can attack creator, performer, or audience, magnetizing any link in the chain of communication described by Socrates in Plato's *Ion*. In some cases, duende flows from the composer, through the interpreter to the listener: a case analogous to the one presented by Socrates: Homer > Ion > the audience. But Lorca cites other cases, "when composer or poet are not worthy of the name, and the interpreter's duende [...] creates a new marvel." The duende touches the second link in the chain, traveling backward in order to give new "lifeblood and art to bodies devoid of expressiveness" (Maurer 1984 40). Like "Imagination, Inspiration, Evasion," Lorca's lecture on duende carries the listener or reader beyond art toward love: "with duende it is easier to love and understand, and one can be *sure* of being loved and understood." All this—a poetics, a defense of Spanish art, art as loving communication—

came fully together in 1933. In 1926, Lorca had praised both Salvador Dalí and the Baroque poet Luis de Góngora—paragon of the imaginative poet—for their sense of limits, their resistance to the "dark forces" of the natural world. By 1933 those "limits" had become limitations (Soria Olmedo) and the perfect poet was a "*disciple* of the elements." In his hunt for the perfect metaphor, the imaginative poet carries a map, Lorca had written in 1926. But seven years later, "neither maps nor exercises can help us search for the duende," only a certain vulnerability, a willingness to look deep inside oneself, and to struggle with the duende "on the rim of the wound" at the edge of death.

As mentioned earlier, both of these lectures have posed problems for editors. Because the manuscript of "Imagination, Inspiration, Evasion" has never been found, it has been reconstructed, little by little, from quotations and summaries in the newspapers of Granada, Madrid, New York and Havana (see "Textual Note"). The recent discovery by Andrew Anderson of the longest and most accurate of those newspaper accounts allows us to publish, in these pages, the most complete version to date and offer a better sense of the restlessly changing poetics of one of Spain's most beloved writers.

Christopher Maurer

MAPPING THE DUENDE

Señoras y Señores:

Desde el año 1918 que ingrese en la Residencia de Estudiantes de Madrid, hasta el 1928 en que la abandone terminado, mis estudios de
filosofia y letras, he oido en aquel refinado salon, donde acudia para corregir su frivolidad de playa francesa ~~mil tardes~~, la vieja aristocracia española ~~xxxxxdxxxxxxxxxx2588x~~cerca de mil conferencias. *tanto que al salir*
Con gana de aire y de sol me ~~he~~ aburrido ~~y~~ me he sentido cubierto por una
leve ceniza casi a punto de convertirse en pimienta de irritacion.

No. Yo no quisiera que entrara en la sala ese terrible moscardon del
aburrimiento que ensarta todas las cabezas por un hilo tenue de sueño
y pone en los ojos de los oyentes unos grupos diminutos de puntas de alfiler.

De modo sencillo con el registro en que mivoz poetica no tiene luces
de madera, ni recodos de cicutas, ni ovejas, que de pronto son cuchillos de ironia,
voy haber si puedo ~~enseñaros una obscura anémonas las que~~ *dentro una sencilla leccion sobre el espiritu oculto de la dolorida* que Don Francisco de
~~Quevedo puso en la cabeza dolorida de España.~~ *España.*

El que está en la piel de toro extendida ~~Jucar~~, *Guadalfeo* ~~xxxxxxx~~, Sil o Pisuerga,
(no quiero citar a los caudales junto ~~xxix~~ *a las ondas color* melena de leon que agita el Plata)
oye decir con medida frecuencia, "esto tiene mucho duende". Manuel Torres,
gran artista del pueblo andaluz, decia a uno que cantaba " Tu tienes voz
tu sabes los estilos pero no triunfaras nunca porque tu notienes duende".

En toda Andalucia, roca de Jaen o caracola de Cadiz, la gente habla constantemente del duende y lo descubre en cuanto sale con instinto
eficaz.

El maravilloso cantaor El Lebrijano creador de la *Debla* decia
"los dias que yo canto con duende, no hay quien pueda conmigo"; la vieja bailarina gitana La Malena ~~wx~~clamó un dia oyendo tocar a Brailousky un fragmento
de Bach"Olé" eso tiene duende" y estuvo aburrida con Gluk y con Brams y con *Rina*
Darius Milhaud ; y Manuel Torres el hombre de mayor cultura en la sangre que

2. First page of a typewritten manuscript of "Juego y teoría del duende," with Lorca's handwritten corrections.

WHEN A SIMPLE LECTURE LIKE "JUEGO Y TEORÍA DEL DUENDE"—A rather brief oral text—gives rise to popular and learned editions, is translated into numerous languages and disseminated in fragments, digitally and in print, for scholars and students in Spain and abroad, I guess we could say that its author has hit the mark. And when readers take over the concept, apply it in casual and rarefied settings, and repeat it ceaselessly until it is almost empty of meaning, we could say that the lecture has hit a nerve. When the word *duende*, and the expression *tener duende*—to have duende—are universally believed to be traditional Spanish expressions and to belong to Spanish folklore but in fact were popularized by Lorca himself, I guess we could say that the author is an alchemist and a master confabulator.

On June 15, 1933, four months before Federico García Lorca first read "Juego y teoría del duende" (Duende: Play and Theory) in Buenos Aires, the Spanish Dance Company of Encarnación López Júlvez, *La Argentinita*, performed in Madrid her version of Manuel de Falla's *The Love Sorcerer*—an event on which she had collaborated with two friends: Lorca and the bullfighter and writer Ignacio Sánchez Mejías. One of the highlights of that evening was the appearance of three nearly seventy-year-old dancers: *La Macarrona, la Malena* and Fernanda Antúnez, divas from the old days of the *café cantante*—the flamenco café. Another of Lorca's friends and accomplices, the Chilean diplomat Carlos Morla Lynch, tells of the occasion in his memoirs. It seemed "the entire intelligentsia" of Madrid was present. Seated beside Morla were the director of the Residencia de Estudiantes, his wife and Morla's, and the young Rafael Rodríguez Rapún, Lorca's secretary and lover. The three old glories came onstage to the click of castanets and an ecstatic ovation. "With their twisted bodies, their wrinkled faces full of stern dignity, their dark lace mantillas and their purple dresses with flounces and long tails, they lift their arms and move their hands with a grace and a presence never to be equaled." Morla compares them to Goya *caprichos* bewitched into dance on a night of sorcery. "The triumph of ugliness, the insuperable beauty of the horrible," Rodríguez Rapún exclaims, as if echoing the Romantic painter Théodore Géricault's idea of "the beauty of the ugly and the exceptional." "Federico applauds furiously," Morla (472) writes, "and howls with enthusiasm. Suddenly he pauses and turns to me: 'Do you like Spain?'"

Despite his immersion in European and Spanish culture of the 1920s and 30s, Morla remains a foreigner and Lorca's question is a little like that of a tour guide pointing out something genuine and perfectly executed, the hidden treasure that the foreigner would not otherwise have understood or admired. "¿Te gusta España?"

And what about us? Do *we* like Spain, the Spain that Lorca believes most legitimate, the Spain whose symbol and cipher is the duende, epitomized by those three old gitanas with gnarled bodies and wrinkled faces, waging their dignified struggle against time, waning skill, and death, but masters of expressiveness and the transmission of emotion?

Perhaps this is the first thing this lecture demands of us: to "like Spain," to comprehend the "enigma of the Spanish soul" (a subtitle Lorca used on occasion), a soul tormented by duende. It is one vision among many, but a vision touched by grace. "Juego y teoría del duende" offers more than what Lorca calls "a simple lesson." It is one of his capital texts, the center and epilogue of his poetics, aspiring to develop a harmonious hypothesis about the arts. It is the essence of a very particular and in many ways original vision of Spanish culture, in which high and low, ancient and modern, go hand in hand, cordially and passionately. And this despite the excesses and stereotypes which the lecture has awakened and multiplied, and for which the poet—with his hyperbole and rhetorical bag of tricks—is only partly to blame.

"Duende: Play and Theory" reveals the ploys of a creator, the legitimate moves of the histrion or poet, juggler or jongleur. On the first page alone are four moments of hocus pocus. In the hand-written manuscript—an X-ray of exaggeration—the poet writes that in the Residencia de Estudiantes he attended "two thousand five hundred lectures," which he then reduces to "one thousand five hundred," and finally to "around a thousand." And then, in a paragraph he ends up crossing out, he claims to have leaped into the Residencia's swimming pool with Salvador Dalí and other young "Residentes," everyone fully clothed, bored silly by the horrendous lecture someone was giving in the salon. In an earlier version, the dive into the pool was a dip in a water channel, a few feet wide, with different actors. Not that the Residencia ever had a swimming pool, or that Lorca ever learned to swim. When, a little later, he mentions four not exactly mighty Spanish rivers—the Júcar, Guadalfeo, Sil and Pisuerga—and tells us—in the 1930s—that within their boundaries and perhaps even in South America people often say, "This really has duende," and that all over Andalusia "people speak constantly of the duende," he is doing so with tongue in cheek. Those expressions were not commonly used that way, either in the 1930s or before, either in dictionaries or in literature. It was *Lorca himself* who was to promote the duende to that popular status. And, finally, when he attributes to Manuel Torre the admonition "you'll never triumph because you have no duende," or the solemn maxim "All that has black sounds has duende," and affirms that the dancer *La Malena*, on hearing the pianist Brailowsky play Bach, once exclaimed "Olé, that has duende," was he quoting correctly? Did *la Malena, el Torre* or el *Lebrijano Viejo* actually say "duende," or did they say "duende*s*"? Singular or plural? Back then, the flamenco artists of southern Andalucia did speak of "duendes," in the plural, but they meant something quite different: first, the ornaments and fioriture of the guitarist and later, the trilling and melismatic flights of the flamenco voice. Like a mischievous goblin, Lorca took pleasure in such camouflage, using recycled materials to build his singular duende—a duende he speaks of as *person*, rooted in the earth, flanked by shadow, wound and struggle, courted only in the presence of death.

The duende existed long before Lorca. Word and concept have their roots in the Spanish Middle Ages, with antecedents in Roman and Islamic mythology. The little genie of Hispanic folklore was both a dark, malefic being and a mischievous trickster with a sense of humor who liked to stir up trouble. The Spanish lexicographer Sebastián de Covarrubias, in his *Tesoro de la lengua castellana o española* (1611) characterized the duende as "one of the spirits who fell with Lucifer, some of whom sank into the depths while others remained in the region of the air and still others on the surface of the earth, as is commonly believed. These last, in houses, mountains, and caves, are apt to frighten people with their appearances, taking on fantastical bodies." Covarrubias informs us of the duende's Latin antecedents—*genii, larvae, lemures, lares*—and offers an etymology of the Spanish word: "for this reason we call them *duendes de casa, dueños de casa* (masters of the house) and, corrupting and shortening the name we say *duendes*." What Covarrubias did not point out was the more than probable crossbreeding of these spirits with their Islamic relatives, the jinn, malignant beings present in the Koran who prowl about in dank and watery places. In fact the jinni is the supernatural being most present in the Islamic world; because its *reality* is confirmed by its presence in the Koran, believers cannot dismiss it as superstition. In his juvenilia Lorca mentions certain duendes (plural) called *martinicos* who used to populate the cisterns and irrigation ditches, pools and fountains of the Albaicín in Granada, a neighborhood which, until the 1960s kept up the impressive network of aljibes (cisterns) constructed by Muslims in the Middle Ages. These traditional duendes, present in many other mythologies, appear with a certain frequency in Lorca's work between 1918 and 1931—for example, in *Amor de don Perlimplín con Belisa en su jardín* (The Love of Don Perlimplín with Belisa In Their Garden) and in his puppet theater. But they have little or nothing to do with the duende of the 1933 lecture.

The demoniacal or demon-like character that Lorca took possession of was once the legendary protagonist of stories told around the fire on winter nights. But the poet drew on other duendes, associated with music, technique, or slang, and these too were sometimes fond of pranks. These were the duendes I referred to earlier, mentioned in 1914 by the musicologist Felipe Pedrell, teacher of the composers Isaac Albéniz and Manuel de Falla. For Pedrell, duendes are fioriture, ornaments, musical phrases on stringed instruments in traditional song or dance. We find this usage, between 1922 and 1935, in the articles of Agustín López Macías, *Galerín*, a popular journalist who wrote for the Sevillian daily *El Liberal*: "wordless trills," melismas, the play of the voice, the melodic filigree frequent in flamenco. The inflexion point occurs in 1929, when Serafín and Joaquín Álvarez Quintero, playwrights with an enormous popular following, latch onto these duendes, which are of common use in the specialized world of Andalusian flamenco but unfamiliar to most speakers of Spanish. When the Quinteros make them the protagonists of their play *Los duendes de Sevilla* (The Duendes of Seville), the duendes are still in the plural, and the Quintero brothers declare them to be exclusively Sevillian, endow them with mysterious, magical, "typically Andalusian" emotional power, and bid them to be fruitful and multiply.

Lorca borrowed certain attributes from these chauvinistic little genies, but carefully covered his tracks. And what else could he do—allow his unfathomable proprietary duende to be associated with the Quintero brothers, the kings of Andalusian kitsch, the lords of local color, the corny joke and crassly commercial theater? Hardly!

In 1929 and 1930 the Quinteros' dreadful little play trickles through the theaters of Spain and crosses the ocean to Buenos Aires and Montevideo, performed there by the company of Lola Membrives. And this is precisely the academic year—1929-30—when Lorca, in the midst of a creative and emotional crisis, leaves for New York. And it is there, in the grid of streets between the Harlem and Hudson rivers, where his duende will begin to germinate—a duende both boldly original and indebted to the duendes that preceded it. Lorca's first reference to the duende occurs in a lecture on flamenco he begins to revise in his dorm room at Columbia University, "Architecture of the Deep Song," an updating of one which he had given in Granada in 1922 to promote the first-ever Festival of Cante Jondo. Lorca's duende comes to life bound to the world of flamenco and will never be separated from it. From that plinth it will attack other arts and disciplines: dance, bullfighting, lyric poetry, music, painting and sculpture—especially religious sculpture—, the writing of the mystics, architecture, popular religion and chant, and the poetry reading. And in fact it was in a reading in 1932 of one of his most difficult books, *Poet in New York*, that Lorca first "invokes" the duende to help his audience "succeed at the hard task of understanding metaphors as soon as they arise, without depending on intelligence or on a critical apparatus, [so as] to capture, as fast as it is read, the rhythmic design of the poem" (*Poet in New York* 182)

In order to profile his duende *de auteur* the poet places him side by side with two metaphors of ancient lineage—the angel and the muse—and contrasts the duende's unrestrained telluric nature with these two illustrious, elegant, luminous airy figures. "Muse and angel come from outside us," he writes. By contrast, "one must awaken the duende in the remotest mansions of the blood." The golden lights projected by the angel, the norms dictated by the muse are lifeless: they enclose the artist in unhealthy formal prisons he must learn not to fear but learn to avoid, for "the true struggle is with the duende," the irrational, deep-dwelling duende. Lorca doesn't say so, but for him the angel and muse are clearly and entirely Apollonian. One can see that he has been feeding on Nietzsche's *The Birth of Tragedy* and endorsing the modern conquest of the Apollonian by the Dionysian. For Lorca, the duende's powers of evasion, its ability to transcend both the wingèd grace of the angel and the intelligent infusions of the muse, are, without a doubt, Dionysian. Above all when it comes to music and dance—the signal arts of this lecture—Lorca follows the Nietzsche who had followed Schopenhauer in his proclamation of music as the archetypal art; in this case a music that cleaves to the voice and the body of the dancer. Both in the lecture and elsewhere, one notices Lorca's commitment to the god of wine, ritual ekstasis and rapture. In March 1935, confirming the Apollonian/Dionysian dichotomy, he writes an introduction for the performance of Pilar López and Rafael Ortega at the Residencia de Estudiantes, and declares that "no one in the world possesses the Dionysian sense of dance of this illustrious Sevillian, radiant honor of Andalusian art, the lovely Pilar, sensual and pure, like the great dancer she is, and the joyful, expressive Rafael Ortega who inspires such deep emotion' (OC iii:259).

And what of the scene Lorca describes in his lecture—when the duende finally possesses Pastora Pavón, *Niña de los Peines* after an exhausting struggle fueled by successive doses of alcohol? (p. 27) Between the lines of Lorca's manuscript, his handwritten pentagram, isn't there an echo of the ecstasy of a Dionysian celebration, "a constantly tempting magic" where "the entire excess of nature [sings] out loudly" and collides—in the words of Nietzsche—with the artifice of a world of "constructed illusion and moderation"? Lorca's anecdote about Pastora Pavón, the emotional epicenter of the lecture and the most frequently quoted and celebrated anecdote in all flamenco literature, was more than probably invented by the poet himself, pulled ingeniously together from bits of reality, things heard, lived, noticed: the refined silverwork or goldwork of a teller of tales. But extremes meet. Lorca once spoke of the material nature of his characters: "They are real, of course. But each real being incarnates a symbol. I try to make my characters into a poetic fact, though I've seen them living and breathing around me. They are an aesthetic reality" (Inglada and Fernández 431-432). And he insisted to journalists, "I conceive of poetry not as an abstraction but as something with a real existence that has happened right beside me. All the people in my poems have actually existed" (*Ibid.* 456). And this applies to the actors the poet brings promiscuously together in a nameless tavern in Cádiz (p. 26): their reality is both corporeal and poetic. Drawn together into a flamenco session, a *juerga*, they demand connoisseurs of cante, and their coterie has a strange ancient nobility—of flamenco, of butchers and of ranchers. They are the select few, acolytes in a cuasi black Mass or mystery cult. The admirable anecdote could be read as a bacchanal, three of whose elements—struggle, alcohol, sacrifice—smear the scene with blood. In reality, the *Guarriros* are from the world of the slaughterhouse; as metaphor, they are presbyters. Murube, a famous breeder of bulls, is also present, with the "air of a Cretan mask," and so is Ignacio Espeleta—another slaughterer—, who is compared to Argantonius, the mythical king of Tartessus, along with a prostitute of flamenco descent, Elvira *la Caliente*, in the flush of her noble blood. And when Pastora manages at last to sing with duende, she sings as though vomiting blood, like a dying bull. The bullfighting circle has been squared on dance floor and gallows.

This unrepeatable scene offers space for reflection about a concept that probably existed before Lorca but to which he gave a name: *música en-duendada*, music with duende, duende music. The duendes of folklore were unmusical little things, disconnected from monody and polyphony. No one ever associated them with eurythmia or song. But the metaphorical duendes that come to life in the Lower Guadalquivir at the beginning of the 20th century—the fioriture and ornaments of guitar and voice—are clearly musical. Lorca gives all this a new, purifying twist by contrasting the duende with the muse and the angel, restoring the duende's enharmonic and inharmonic propensities; better said, its capacity for broken, stripped-down sound. The angel and muse are philharmonic creatures, like human beings. The angels sing and dance eternally in unison, in antiphonal style, rendering homage to God on his throne, while the muses in their exclusive Olympian gatherings intone sweet melodies to Father Zeus, praising him and the rest of his far-flung family. When the *Niña de los Peines*, exhausted by an intense struggle against forms, is driven to "tear her voice," impoverish her skills and security, and offer "not forms, but the marrow of form," she claims that bodily space for the voice. The same operation is evident in another of Lorca's anecdotes, the dance competition in Jerez de la Frontera won by an eighty-year-old woman who defeats lovely girls and boys with waists supple as water merely by "raising her arms, throwing back her head and stamping her foot." (p. 28) Flamenco with duende is flamenco in the bones, almost without song. Dance with duende is dance suspended and close to exhaustion. In both, expressiveness and frankness triumph regally over technique.

In this as in other forays into the exclusive fields of flamenco, dance, and the bullfight, García Lorca allowed himself to be counseled and guided by a pair of experts, Ignacio Sánchez Mejías and his lover the dancer, actress and singer *La Argentinita*, who put him in touch with some of the greatest artists of his time and introduced him to the dancer Rafael Ortega Monge. Rafael, the descendant of glorious gitano flamenco artists and bullfighters, must have fascinated Lorca with his scuttlebutt and witty stories, some of which found their way into this lecture. We can attribute the legendary history of the *Guarriros* and of the clever little fellow who taunted *Niña de los Peines* ("*Viva* Paris!") to the repertoire of Ortega. Some of the lecture's many references to bull-fighting can be traced to the lessons imparted by Ignacio Sánchez Mejías to his young friend and to the lecture he gave on February 20, 1930 at Columbia University, "El pase de la muerte" (The Pass of Death), where he was introduced by Federico himself. But neither advice nor influence was unidirectional. The creative trio Lorca-*La Argentinita*-Sánchez Mejías is the Andalusian answer to another, better known and more closely scrutinized threesome—one more sharply focused on the avant-garde: that of Lorca, Buñuel, Dalí.

Once Lorca had drawn the firm outline of his singular duende, he infused its empty spaces with the sombre and secret, the agonistic and incomprehensible, the uninhibited and ecstatic, and did so with an imposing array of rhetorical resources: emphatic asseverations, persistent prosopopoeia, personification, parables, abundant hyperbole, carefully applied color and landscaping... Despite the lecture's apparent amenity, Lorca's palette is distinctly black and red. Black comes first, in the metaphor of the "black sounds," the mantra or basso continuo of the lecture and of flamencology. While total darkness is mentioned explicitly and often, the second essential color is not named at all, though it is latently and overwhelmingly everywhere. It is in the blood that seeps into and eclipses every inch of the duende's fabric. It is in the flame, the slaughterhouse, the prostitute, the wound, volcanoes, wings of rusty knives, Mudejar bricks, and a "landscape of blood and sand," a term which, according to the historian Francisco Calvo Serraller (48-49), "is usually associated with the bullfight but which, in reality takes us back to a much more atavistic background, that of sacrificial rites." The allegorical connections of blood lead us toward a pulsing, combative, fiery horizon of vermilion (symbolic color of Dionysus) but also toward an earthen, mineral, inert one, the province of Saturn, the color of a dark plum.

After he has engendered his symbolic creature, Lorca begins to dress it. But the dressing of the duende did not end with the lecture, it is still going on. Lorca's duende has never ceased to generate images, try on different costumes, lend itself to explication, interpretation, adoption, and to find new range and play in fields as diverse as theater, music, narrative, anecdote, flamenco—including the crudest sort of flamenco, pitched to mass tourism—as well as flamencology, spinning out cliché and digression and wandering off toward the almost total exhaustion of meaning.

Lorca's ambitious lesson aimed to be an essay on all of the arts, a harmonious theory of the aesthetic act, but perhaps because his referential apparatus, his array of examples, names and landscapes, focus on the bullfight and above all on flamenco, the lecture has gotten its truest reception in those fields. The world of flamenco embraced and adopted Lorca's duende like its own child and responded to the system of ideas that are present or latent in Lorca's text: ideas of purity and incorruptibility, rejection of commercialized, professionalized flamenco, the gitano presence, a hermetic "oriental" antiquity, the prestige of the ruin, the beauty of ugliness, the authenticity to be found in the warm, intimate, reserved and discriminating sanctum of the *juerga*, and a marked preference for the serious, the hoarse, the crude, the raw, the scorched. And the river of duende will meander semantically onward.

"I shall try to give you a simple lesson in the hidden, aching spirit of Spain," the poet says at the beginning of his lecture, and he gives that furtive spirit a name. To contemplate that spirit, and that ineffable creature, one needs distance, perspective and well-paced, honest speech. The distance was both speculative and physical (Lorca was speaking in Buenos Aires), at a time when human space still tracked faithfully with human time. New irradiations of duende may well be in progress—new ways to identify the emotional transfusion that can transport an audience to a higher plane of sympathetic understanding. Here, based on a critical annotated edition of the original, is a fresh translation into English, a language spoken where Lorca began to find his way toward duende, and where it continues to inspire and thrive.

José Javier León

DUENDE: PLAY AND THEORY

3. *Fabulous Beast Approaching a House.* New York, ca. 1929-1930, the years Lorca was lecturing on "Imagination, Inspiration, Evasion" and the "hecho poético" (poetic fact or event), of which this drawing might serve as an example. India ink and crayon on paper. From the poet's private collection, preserved by Francisco García Lorca and inherited by Gloria García-Lorca de los Ríos, Madrid.

From 1918, when I entered the Residencia de Estudiantes de Madrid[1,] until 1928, when I finished my studies in Philosophy and Letters and left, I attended, in that elegant salon where the old Spanish aristocracy did penance for its frivolous seaside vacations in France, around one thousand lectures.[2]

Hungry for fresh air and sunlight, I used to get so bored that I felt myself covered in a film of ash that might turn at any moment into sneezing powder.

So no—I won't let into this room the terrible botfly of boredom that can string heads together on the fine thread of sleep and make the eyes prickle with tiny pins and needles.[3]

As simply as possible, in the register of my poetic voice that has neither the sheen of wood[4] nor twists of hemlock, nor sheep who suddenly turn into knives of irony, I shall try to give you a simple lesson in the hidden, aching spirit of Spain.

Whoever finds himself on the bull's hide[5] stretched between the Júcar, Guadalfeo, Sil or Pisuerga rivers, not to mention the great waters—the color of a lion's mane—churned up by the Plata,[6] often hears people say, "This really has duende."[7] Manuel Torres,[8] great artist of the Andalusian people, once told a singer, "You have a voice, you know the styles, but you'll never triumph, because you have no duende."

All over Andalusia—rock of Jaén or whorled shell of Cádiz—people speak constantly of the duende, and identify it accurately and instinctively wherever it appears.[9]

The marvelous singer *El Lebrijano*, creator of the debla,[10] used to say, "On days when I sing with duende, no one can touch me." Hearing Brailowsky play some Bach[11] the old gitana dancer *La Malena*[12] once exclaimed, "Olé! That has duende!" But she was bored by Gluck, Brahms, and Darius Milhaud.[13] Manuel Torres, who had more culture in the blood than any man I ever met, pronounced this splendid sentence on hearing Falla himself play his nocturne *In the Generalife*:[14] "All that has black sounds has duende."[15] And there is no greater truth.

These black sounds are the mystery, the roots that fasten in the silt we all know and all ignore, the fertile silt that gives us the very substance of art. "Black sounds," said that man of the Spanish people, concurring with Goethe, who defined duende while speaking of Paganini: "A mysterious power which everyone feels and no philosopher explains."[16]

The duende, then, is a power, not a work. It is struggle, not thought. I have heard an old maestro of the guitar say, "The duende is not in the throat; the duende climbs up inside you, from the soles of the feet."[17] Meaning this: it is not a question of ability, but of true, living style, of blood, of the most ancient culture, but also of creation enacted in the moment.

This "mysterious power which everyone feels and no philosopher explains" is, in sum, the spirit of the earth. It is the duende that scorched the heart of Nietzsche, who searched in vain for its external forms on the Rialto Bridge[18] and in the music of Bizet,[19] without finding it and without realizing that the duende he was pursuing had leaped straight from the Greek mysteries to the dancers of Cádiz or the decapitated Dionysian cry of Silverio's siguiriya.[20]

But I do not want anyone to confuse the duende with the theological demon of doubt at whom Luther, on a Bacchic impulse, hurled a pot of ink in Nuremberg,[21] or with the destructive and rather stupid Catholic devil who disguises himself as a bitch to get into convents,[22] or with the talking monkey carried by Cervantes' Malgesí in his comedy entitled *Jealousy and the Forests of Ardennes*.[23] No.

The dark, shuddering duende I am talking about descends from the joyful marble-and-salt demon of Socrates—the demon who scratched at him angrily on the day he swallowed the hemlock—and from the melancholy little demon of Descartes: a demon small as a green almond, who, sick of circles and lines, went off to the canals to listen to the singing of big blurry sailors.[24]

Every man and every artist, whether he is Nietzsche or Cézanne, climbs each step in the tower of his perfection by fighting his duende, not his angel, as it has been said, or his muse. We must make this fundamental distinction, at the very root of the work.

The angel guides and gives like Saint Raphael, defends and avoids like Saint Michael, announces and foretells like Saint Gabriel.[25]

The angel dazzles, but flies high over a man's head, shedding his grace, and the man effortlessly realizes his work or his charm or his dance. The angel on the road to Damascus,[26] the one that came through the crack of the little balcony at Assisi,[27] and the one who tracked Heinrich Suso[28] *command*, and there is no way to resist their lights, for they beat their steel wings in an atmosphere of predestination.

The muse dictates and sometimes prompts. She can do relatively little, and by now she is so distant and so tired (I have seen her twice) that she had to be given half a heart of marble. Muse poets hear voices and don't know where they are coming from, but they are coming from the muse that encourages them and sometimes snacks on them, as happened to Apollinaire, a great poet destroyed by the horrible muse who appears with him in a certain painting by the divine, angelic Rousseau.[29] The muse awakens the intelligence, bringing landscapes of columns and a false taste of laurel, but intelligence is often the enemy of poetry, because it limits too much, and it elevates the poet to a sharp-edged throne where he forgets that ants could eat him or that a big arsenic lobster could fall suddenly on his head—things against which the muses that live in monocles and in the lukewarm, lacquered roses of tiny salons are quite helpless.[30]

Muse and angel come from outside us: the angel gives lights, and the muse gives forms (Hesiod learned from her).[31] Gold leaf or tunic fold: the poet receives norms in his copse of laurel.[32] But one must awaken the duende in the remotest mansions of the blood. And reject the angel, and give the muse a kick in the seat of the pants, and conquer our fear of the violet smile exhaled by eighteenth-century poetry, and of the great telescope in whose lens the muse, sickened by limits, is sleeping.

The true struggle is with the duende.

We know the roads to search for God. From the barbarous way of the hermit to the subtle one of the mystic. With a tower like Saint Teresa or with the three ways of Saint John of the Cross.[33] And though we may have to cry out in the voice of Isaiah, "Truly thou art a hidden God,"[34] in the end God sends each seeker his first fiery thorns.[35]

But neither maps nor exercises can help us search for the duende. We only know that he burns the blood like an ointment of broken glass,[36] that he exhausts, that he rejects all the sweet geometry we have learned,

that he smashes styles, that he leans on the human pain that has no consolation and makes Goya (master of the grays, silvers, and pinks of the
finest English painting) work with his fists and knees in horrible bitu-
mens.[37] He strips Mossèn Cinto Verdauger in the cold of the Pyrenees[38]
or leads Jorge Manrique to await death in the barrens of Ocaña[39], or
dresses Rimbaud's delicate body in the green suit of a saltimbanque,[40] or
puts the eyes of a dead fish on the Comte de Lautréamont in the early
hours of the boulevard.[41]

The great artists of the south of Spain, gitanos or flamencos, whether
they sing, play or dance, know that there can be no emotion until the duende arrives. They fool people into thinking they have duende—authors
and painters and literary fashionmongers cheat you like that every day—
but we have only to pay a little attention and not surrender to indifference in order to discover their tricks and chase away their clumsy artifice.

The Andalusian singer Pastora Pavón, *La Niña de los Peines*,[42] dark
Hispanic genius whose powers of fantasy are equal to those of Goya or
Rafael *el Gallo*,[43] was once singing in a little tavern in Cádiz. For a while
she played with her voice of shadow, of molten tin, her moss-covered
voice, braiding it into her hair or soaking it in *manzanilla*[44] and letting it
wander away to the farthest, darkest bramble patches. No use. Nothing.
The audience remained silent.

In the same room was Ignacio Espeleta, handsome as a Roman tor-
toise, who had once been asked, "How come you don't work?" and had
answered, with a smile worthy of Argantonius, "Why should I? I'm
from Cádiz!"[45] There, too, was Elvira *la Caliente*, aristocratic Sevillian
whore, direct descendant of Soledad Vargas who in [19]30 refused to
marry a Rothschild because he was not her equal in blood.[46] And the
Guarriros,[47] whom people take to be butchers but who are really millen-
nial priests still sacrificing bulls to Geryon.[48] And in one corner sat the
formidable bull rancher Don Pablo Murube, with the air of a Cretan
mask.[49] When Pastora Pavón finished singing there was total silence,
until a tiny man, one of those dancing, prancing little homunculi who
rise suddenly out of brandy bottles, murmured "*Viva* Paris!"[50] As if to
say: "Here we care nothing about ability, technique, skill. What matters
to us is something else."

As though crazy, torn like a medieval mourner, *La Niña de los Peines* leapt to her feet, tossed off a glass of burning *cazalla*,[51] and sat down to sing with a scorched throat: without voice, without breath or nuance, but with duende. She was able to kill all the scaffolding of the song and leave way for a furious, enslaving duende, friend of sand winds, who made the listeners rip their clothes almost with the same rhythm as the blacks of the Antilles when, in the lucumí rite, they huddle before the image of Santa Bárbara.[52]

La Niña de los Peines had to tear her voice because she knew she had an exquisite audience, one which demanded not forms but the marrow of form, pure music with a body lean enough to stay in the air. She had to impoverish her skill and her security, send away her muse and become helpless, that her duende might come and deign to fight her hand-to-hand. And how she sang! Her voice was no longer playing. It was a jet of blood worthy—given her pain[53] and her sincerity—to blossom like a ten-fingered hand around the nailed but stormy feet of a Christ by Juan de Juni.[54]

The duende's arrival always means a radical change in all the forms. It infuses old planes with unknown feelings of freshness and the quality of something newly and miraculously created that brings about an almost religious enthusiasm.[55]

In all Arabic music, whether dance, song, or elegy, the duende's arrival is greeted with energetic cries of Allah! Allah!—God, God!—which is so close to the *Olé* of the bullfight that who knows if it isn't the same thing?[56] And in all the songs of southern Spain the duende is greeted with sincere cries of ¡Viva Dios!—deep tender human cry of communication with God through the five senses, thanks to the duende, who roils the body and voice of the dancer.[57] It is a real and poetic evasion of this world, as pure as that of the strange seventeenth-century poet Pedro Soto de Rojas with his seven gardens[58], or that John Climacus with his tremulous ladder of tears.[59]

Naturally, when this evasion succeeds, everyone feels its effects, both the initiate, who sees how style has conquered a poor material, and the unenlightened, who feels some sort of inexpressible but authentic emotion. Years ago, an eighty-year-old woman won first prize at a dance contest in Jerez de la Frontera. She was competing against beautiful women and boys with waists supple as water, and all she did was raise her arms, throw back her head, and stamp her foot on the floor. In such a gathering of muses and angels—beauty of form, beauty of smile—it was that moribund duende that had to triumph, sweeping the floor with wings of rusty knives.[60]

All the arts are capable of duende, but where it finds greatest range, naturally, is in music, dance, and spoken poetry, for these require a living body to interpret them, being forms that perpetually come to life and die, raising their contours against an exact present. Often the duende of the composer passes into the duende of the interpreter, and at other times, when a composer or poet is no such thing, the interpreter's duende—this is interesting—creates a new marvel that resembles, but is not, the primitive form. This was the case of Eleonora Duse, possessed by duende, who looked for plays that had failed so she could make them triumph thanks to her own inventions[61], and the case of Paganini, as explained by Goethe, who made one hear deep melodies in vulgar trifles[62], and the case of a delightful girl I saw in Puerto de Santa María singing and dancing that horrible, corny Italian song "Oh Mari!" with such rhythms, silences, and intention, that she turned the Neapolitan gewgaw into a hard serpent of chased gold.[63] What happened was that these people had found something new and unprecedented that could give lifeblood and art to bodies devoid of expressiveness.

All of the arts and in fact all countries are capable of duende, angel, and muse. And just as Germany has, with few exceptions, muse, and Italy shall always have angel, so in all ages Spain is moved by duende, for it is a country of music and ancient dances where the duende squeezes the lemons of dawn—a country of death, open to death.

In every other country death is an end. Death comes, and they close the curtains. Not in Spain. In Spain they open them. Many Spaniards live indoors until the day they die and are carried out into the sunlight. A dead man in Spain is more alive as a dead man than anyplace else on earth. His profile wounds like the edge of a barber's razor.[64] The joke about death or its silent contemplation are familiar to every Spaniard. From Quevedo's "Dream of the Skulls" to Valdés Leal's *Putrescent Archbishop*,[65] from seventeenth-century Marbella who says, as she dies giving birth in the middle of the road:

La sangre de mis entrañas	Blood from my entrails
cubriendo el caballo está.	is covering the horse.
Las patas de tu caballo	Your horse's hoofs
echan fuego de alquitrán…	strike fire from pitch…[66]

to the more recent youth of Salamanca who is killed by a bull and moans:

Amigos, que yo me muero;	Friends, I'm dying.
amigos, yo estoy muy malo.	friends, it's pretty bad.
Tres pañuelos tengo dentro,	Three handkerchiefs in me,
y este que meto son cuatro…	and this one makes a fourth…[67]

stretches a balustrade of saltpeter flowers where the Spanish people go to contemplate death.[68] To one side, the more rugged one, are the verses of Jeremiah,[69] and to the other, more lyrical, is an aromatic cypress.[70] But throughout the country, everything that is most important finds its final, metallic valuation in death.[71]

The chasuble and the window and the cart wheel and the pocket knife and the prickly beards of the shepherds and the naked moon and the fly and moist pantry shelves and demolished buildings and lace-covered saints and quicklime and the wounding edges of eaves and miradors possess, in Spain, fine herbs and weeds of death, the allusions and murmurings (perceptible to any alert spirit) that fill our memory with the stale air of our own passing. It is no accident that so much of Spanish art is tied to the land, all thistles and boundary stones. The lamentation of Pleberio,[72] the dances of Maestro Josef María de Valdivielso[73] are not isolated examples, and it is hardly a matter of chance that this beloved resembles no other in Europe:

Si tú eres mi linda amiga,	If you are my pretty friend,
¿cómo no me miras, di?	why don't you look at me?
Ojos con que te miraba	The eyes I looked at you with
a la sombra se los di.	I have given to the dark.
Si tú eres mi linda amiga,	If you are my pretty friend,
¿cómo no me besas, di?	why don't you kiss me?
Labios con que te besaba	The lips I kissed you with
a la tierra se los di.	I have given to the earth.

Si tú eres mi linda amiga	If you are my pretty friend,
¿cómo no me abrazas, di?	why don't you hold me tight?
Brazos con que te abrazaba	The arms I hugged you with
de gusanos los cubrí.	I have covered in worms.[74]

nor is it strange that this song is heard at the very dawn of our lyric poetry:

Dentro del vergel	In the garden
moriré,	I will die.
dentro del rosal	Among the roses
matar me han.	they will kill me.
Yo me iba, mi madre,	I was going, mother,
las rosas coger,	to pick roses,
hallara la muerte	and would find death
dentro del vergel.	in the garden.
Yo me iba, madre,	I was going, mother,
las rosas cortar,	to cut roses,
hallara la muerte	and would find death
dentro del rosal.	among the roses.
Dentro del vergel	In the garden
moriré,	I will die,
dentro del rosal	among the roses
matar me han.	they will kill me. [75]

The moon-frozen heads painted by Zurbarán,[76] the yellows of El Greco—color of lightning or rancid lard—, the narrative of Father Sigüenza,[77] the entire work of Goya, the presbytery of the church of the Escorial,[78] all polychrome sculpture, the crypt of the house of the Duke of Osuna,[79] the "Death with a Guitar" in the chapel of the Benaventes at Medina de Rioseco[80]—all these mean the same, in high culture, as the processions of San Andrés de Teixido, where the dead play a role,[81] the dirges sung by Asturian women with flame-filled lanterns in the November night,[82] the song and dance of the Sibyl in the cathedrals of Mallorca and Toledo,[83] the dark "In *record*" of Tortosa,[84] and the countless rites of Good Friday which, along with the supremely civilized festival of the bullfight,[85] form the popular triumph of Spanish death. In all the world, only Mexico can go hand in hand with my country.

When the muse sees death arrive, she shuts the door or raises a plinth or promenades an urn and writes an epitaph with waxen hand, but soon she is watering her laurel again in a silence that wavers between two breezes. Beneath the broken arch of the ode, she pieces together with funereal feeling the exact flowers of fifteenth-century Italian painters, and calls on Lucretius's trusty rooster to chase away unforeseen shades.[86]

When the angel sees death approach, he flies in slow circles and weaves tears of narcissus and ice into the elegy we have seen trembling in the hands of Keats, Villasandino, Herrera, Bécquer, and Juan Ramón Jiménez.[87] But how it horrifies the angel to feel even the tiniest spider on his tender rosy foot!

And the duende? The duende does not come at all unless he sees that death is possible. The duende must know beforehand that he can serenade death's house, that he can rock those branches we all bear— branches that do not have, will never have, any consolation.

With idea, sound, or gesture, the duende likes to fight the creator on the very rim of the well. Angel and muse escape with violin or compass, but the duende wounds, and in the healing of that wound, which never closes, lie the strange, invented qualities of a man's work.

The magical virtue of a poem is to remain possessed by duende so that it can baptize in dark water all who look at it, for with duende it is easier to love and understand, and one can be *sure* of being loved and understood. In poetry this struggle for expression and the communication of expression is sometimes mortal.

Recall the case of Saint Teresa, that supremely "flamenco" woman so full of duende. "Flamenca" not because she tied up a furious bull and gave it three magnificent passes (which she did!) and not because she thought herself very lovely in presence of Fray Juan de la Miseria,[88] or because she slapped the papal nuncio, but because she was one of the few creatures whose duende—not angel, for the angel never attacks—transfixed her with a dart and wanted to kill her for having stolen his deepest secret: the subtle bridge between the five senses and the center of raw, live flesh, cloud or sea of Love freed from Time.[89]

Most valiant conqueror of the duende, the opposite of Phillip of Austria, who pined after the muse and angel in theology and was finally imprisoned by a duende of freezing ardor in the work of the Escorial, where geometry borders on dream and the duende dons the mask of a muse to the eternal punishment of that great king.[90]

We have said that the duende loves the rim of the wound, and that he draws near places where forms fuse together into a yearning superior to their visible expression.

In Spain, as among the people of the Orient, where the dance is religious expression, the duende has unlimited range over the bodies of the dancers of Cádiz, praised by Martial, over the breasts of singers, praised by Juvenal, and in the liturgy of the bulls, an authentic religious drama where, as in the Mass, a God is sacrificed to and adored.[91]

It is as though all the duende of the classical world had crowded into this perfect festival, revealing the culture, the acute sensibility of a people who discover man's best anger, bile, and tears. Neither in Spanish dance nor in the bullfight does anyone amuse himself. The duende takes it upon himself to make us suffer by means of a drama of living forms, and prepares the stairways for an evasion of the surrounding reality.[92]

The duende works on the body of the dancer as the wind works on sand. His magical power turns a girl into a lunar paralytic, or gives the blush of an adolescent to the broken old man begging in the wine shop,[93] or makes a woman's hair smell like a port at night,[94] and he works continuously on the arms with expressions that give birth to the dances of every age.[95]

But he can never repeat himself. This is interesting to emphasize. The duende doesn't repeat himself, any more do the forms of the sea during a squall.

The duende is at his most impressive in the bullfight, for he must fight both death, which can destroy him, and geometry—measurement, the very basis of the festival.

The bull has his orbit, and the bullfighter has his, and between these two orbits is a point of danger, the vertex of the terrible play.

You can have muse with the *muleta* and angel with the *banderillas* and pass for a good bullfighter, but in the capework, when the bull is still clean of wounds, and at the moment of the kill, you need the duende's help to achieve artistic truth.[96]

The bullfighter who scares the audience with his bravado is not bullfighting, but has ridiculously reduced himself to doing what anyone can do: *risking his life*. But the torero bitten by duende gives a lesson in Pythagorean music and makes us forget he is always tossing his own heart over the bull's horns.[97]

From the half-shadow of the ring, Lagartijo with his Roman duende, Joselito with his Jewish duende, Belmonte with his baroque duende, and Cagancho with his gitano duende show poets, painters, musicians, and composers, the four great roads of Spanish tradition.[98]

Spain is the only country where death is a national spectacle and where death sounds long trumpet blasts at the coming of spring, and Spanish art is always ruled by a shrewd duende who makes it different and inventive.

The duende who, for the first time in sculpture, smears blood on the cheeks of the saints of Maestro Mateo de Compostela[99] is the same one that makes Saint John of the Cross weep or burns naked nymphs in the religious sonnets of Lope.[100]

The duende that raises the tower of Sahagún or bakes hot bricks in Calatayud or Teruel[101] is the same one who breaks the clouds of El Greco and kicks into flight the constables of Quevedo and chimeras of Goya.[102]

When it rains, he brings duende-ridden Velázquez out from behind the monarchic grays where he is hiding. When it snows, he makes Herrera strip naked to show that the cold does not kill[103]. When it is burning hot, he shoves Berruguete into the flames and makes him invent a new space for sculpture.[104]

The muse of Góngora and the angel of Garcilaso must let go of their laurel garlands when the duende of Saint John of the Cross comes by and

| el ciervo vulnerado | the wounded stag |
| por el otero asoma | appears on the hill[105] |

The muse of Gonzalo de Berceo and the angel of Arcipreste de Hita must make way for Jorge Manrique, mortally wounded at the doors of the castle of Belmonte.[106] The muse of Gregorio Hernández and the angel of José de Mora must yield to the duende (crying tears of blood) of Pedro de Mena and to the duende (with the head of an Assyrian bull) of Martínez Montañés[107]; just as the melancholy muse of Catalonia and the drizzly angel of Galicia—muse and angel of warm bread and gentle cow—behold with love and wonder the duende of Castile with his norms of clean scrubbed sky and arid land.

Duende of Quevedo and duende of Cervantes,[108] one with green anemones of phosphorus and the other with blossoms of Ruidera gypsum,[109] crown the altarpiece of the duende of Spain.[110]

Each art has a duende different in form and style, but their roots are joined at the source of the black sounds of Manuel Torres—the essential, uncontrollable, quivering, common base of wood, sound, canvas, and word.[111]

Behind those black sounds, tenderly and intimately, live volcanoes, ants, zephyrs and the huge night, pressing its waist against the Milky Way.

Ladies and gentlemen: I have raised three arches, and with clumsy hand have placed in them the muse, the angel, and the duende.

The muse stays still. She can have a minutely folded tunic or cow eyes like the ones that stare at us in Pompeii or the huge, four-faced nose given to her by her great friend Picasso.[112] The angel can ruffle the hair of Antonello da Messina, the tunic of Lippi,[113] and the violin of Masolino[114] or Rousseau.[115]

The duende... Where is the duende? Through the empty arch comes a wind, a mental wind blowing relentlessly over the heads of the dead, in search of new landscapes and unknown accents; a wind that smells of baby's spittle, crushed grass, and jellyfish veil, announcing the constant baptism of newly created things.

JUEGO Y TEORÍA DEL DUENDE

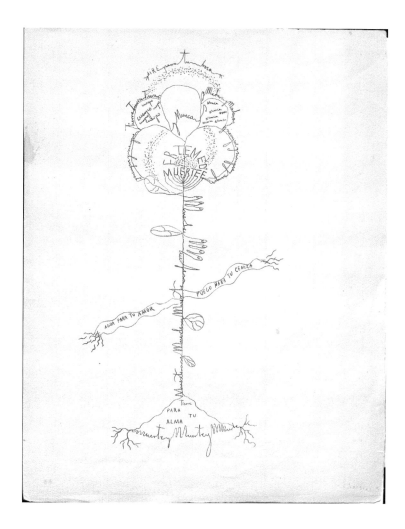

Rosa de la muerte. Caligrama / Rose of Death. Calligram. Blue ink on paper.
Drawing printed on the end-leaf of a limited edition of Ricardo E. Molinari's
poem *Una rosa para Stefan George* (A Rose for Stefan George), printed
in Buenos Aires by Francisco A. Colombo in 1934, during Lorca's visit to
Argentina. The German poet had died a few months earlier. Copy 42, inscribed
"For Laurita de los Ríos", and signed "Federico" and "Ricardo E. Molinari".
According to Mario Hernández (*Libro de los dibujos*) Lorca's drawing "seems to
respond to the following verses from the Molinari poem: 'Sleep. It is good to
sleep forever, next to the sea; / the dry rivers under the earth with their rose
of dead blood." Lorca's text reads in part, "Air for your mouth," "Water for your
Love," "Fire for your Ash," "Earth for your soul." For a complete transcription
see Hernández. Cat 291, Centro Federico García Lorca.

Desde el año 1918, que ingresé en la Residencia de Estudiantes de Madrid, hasta el 1928 en que la abandoné, terminados mis estudios de Filosofía y Letras, he oído en aquel refinado salón, donde acudía para corregir su frivolidad de playa francesa la vieja aristocracia española, cerca de mil conferencias.

Con gana de aire y de sol me he aburrido tanto que, al salir, me he sentido cubierto por una leve ceniza casi a punto de convertirse en pimienta de irritación.

No. Yo no quisiera que entrara en la sala ese terrible moscardón del aburrimiento que ensarta todas las cabezas por un hilo tenue de sueño y pone en los ojos de los oyentes unos grupos diminutos de puntas de alfiler.

De modo sencillo, con el registro en que mi voz poética no tiene luces de madera, ni recodos de cicutas, ni ovejas que de pronto son cuchillos de ironía, voy a ver si puedo daros una sencilla lección sobre el espíritu oculto de la dolorida España.

El que está en la piel de toro extendida, Júcar, Guadalfeo, Sil o Pisuerga (no quiero citar a los caudales junto a las ondas color melena de león que agita el Plata), oye decir con medida frecuencia: «Esto tiene mucho duende». Manuel Torres, gran artista del pueblo andaluz, decía a uno que cantaba: «Tú tienes voz, tú sabes los estilos, pero no triunfarás nunca porque tú no tienes duende».

En toda Andalucía, roca de Jaén o caracola de Cádiz, la gente habla constantemente del duende y lo descubre en cuanto sale con instinto eficaz.

El maravilloso cantaor el Lebrijano, creador de la debla, decía: «Los días que yo canto con duende, no hay quien pueda conmigo»; la vieja bailarina gitana la Malena exclamó un día oyendo tocar a Brailowsky un fragmento de Bach: «¡Olé, eso tiene duende!» y estuvo aburrida con Gluck y con Brahms y con Darius Milhaud; y Manuel Torres, el hombre de mayor cultura en la sangre que yo he conocido, dijo escuchando al propio Falla su *Nocturno del Generalife* esta espléndida frase: «Todo lo que tiene sonidos negros tiene duende». Y no hay verdad más grande.

Estos sonidos negros son el misterio, las raíces que se clavan en el limo que todos conocemos, que todos ignoramos, pero de donde nos llega lo que es substancial en el arte. Sonidos negros, dijo el hombre popular de España, y coincidió con Goethe, que hace la definición del duende al hablar de Paganini, diciendo: «Poder misterioso que todos sienten y ningún filósofo explica».

Así pues, el duende es un poder y no un obrar, es un luchar y no un pensar. Yo he oído decir a un viejo maestro guitarrista: «El duende no está en la garganta, el duende sube por dentro, desde las plantas de los pies». Es decir, no es cuestión de facultad, sino de verdadero estilo vivo; es decir, de sangre; es decir, de viejísima cultura y a la vez de creación en acto.

Este «poder misterioso que todos sienten y que ningún filósofo explica» es, en suma, el espíritu de la Tierra, el mismo duende que abrasó el corazón de Nietzsche, que lo buscaba en sus formas exteriores sobre el puente Rialto o en la música de Bizet, sin encontrarlo y sin saber que el duende que él perseguía había saltado de los misterios griegos a las bailarinas de Cádiz o al dionisíaco grito degollado de la siguiriya de Silverio.

Así pues, no quiero que nadie confunda el duende con el demonio teológico de la duda, al que Lutero, con un sentimiento báquico, le arrojó un frasco de tinta en Nüremberg, ni con el diablo católico, destructor y poco inteligente, que se disfraza de perra para entrar en los conventos, ni con el mono parlante que lleva el Malgesí de Cervantes en la *Comedia de los celos y las selvas de Ardenia*. No.

El duende de que hablo, obscuro y estremecido, es descendiente de aquel alegrísimo demonio de Sócrates, mármol y sal, que lo arañó indignado el día que tomó la cicuta, y del otro melancólico demonillo de Descartes, pequeño como una almendra verde, que, harto de círculos y líneas, salía por los canales para oír cantar a los grandes marineros borrosos.

Todo hombre, todo artista, llámese Nietzsche o Cézanne, cada escala que sube en la torre de su perfección es a costa de la lucha que sostiene con su duende, no con su ángel, como se ha dicho, ni con su musa. Es preciso hacer esta distinción, fundamental para la raíz de la obra.

El ángel guía y regala como san Rafael, defiende y evita como san Miguel, anuncia y previene como san Gabriel.

El ángel deslumbra, pero vuela sobre la cabeza del hombre, está por encima, derrama su gracia y el hombre sin ningún esfuerzo realiza su obra, o su simpatía o su danza. El ángel del camino de Damasco y el que entra por la rendija del balconcillo de Asís, o el que sigue los pasos de Enrique Susón, *ordenan* y no hay modo de oponerse a sus luces, porque agitan sus alas de acero en el ambiente del predestinado.

La musa dicta, y en algunas ocasiones sopla. Puede relativamente poco porque ya está lejana y tan cansada (yo la he visto dos veces), que tuvieron que ponerle medio corazón de mármol. Los poetas de musa oyen voces y no saben dónde, pero son de la musa que los alienta y a veces se los merienda, como en el caso de Apollinaire, gran poeta destruido por la horrible musa con que lo pintó el divino angélico Rousseau. La musa despierta la inteligencia, trae paisajes de columnas y falso sabor de laureles, y la inteligencia es muchas veces la enemiga de la poesía, porque limita demasiado, porque eleva al poeta en un trono de agudas aristas, y le hace olvidar que de pronto se lo pueden comer las hormigas o le puede caer en la cabeza una gran langosta de arsénico contra la cual no pueden las musas que viven en los monóculos o en la rosa de tibia laca del pequeño salón.

Ángel y musa vienen de fuera; el ángel da luces y la musa formas (Hesíodo aprendió de ella). Pan de oro o pliegue de túnica, el poeta recibe normas en su bosquecillo de laureles. En cambio, al duende hay que despertarlo en las últimas habitaciones de la sangre; y rechazar al ángel, y dar un puntapié a la musa, y perder el miedo a la sonrisa de violetas que exhala la poesía del XVIII y al gran telescopio en cuyos cristales se duerme la musa enferma de límites.

La verdadera lucha es con el duende.

Se saben los caminos para buscar a Dios. Desde el modo bárbaro del eremita al modo sutil del místico. Con una torre como Santa Teresa o con tres caminos como San Juan de la Cruz. Y aunque tengamos que clamar con voz de Isaías: «Verdaderamente tú eres Dios escondido», al fin y al cabo Dios manda al que lo busca sus primeras espinas de fuego.

Para buscar al duende no hay mapa ni ejercicio. Solo se sabe que quema la sangre como un trópico de vidrios, que agota, que rechaza toda la dulce geometría aprendida, que rompe los estilos, que se apoya en el dolor humano que no tiene consuelo, que hace que Goya, maestro en los grises, en los platas y en los rosas de la mejor pintura inglesa, pinte con las rodillas y los puños con horribles negros de betún; o desnuda a mosén Cinto Verdaguer en el frío de los Pirineos, o lleva a Jorge Manrique a esperar a la muerte en el páramo de Ocaña, o viste con un traje verde de saltimbanqui el cuerpo delicado de Rimbaud, o pone ojos de pez muerto al Conde de Lautréamont en la madrugada del boulevard.

Los grandes artistas del sur de España, gitanos o flamencos, ya canten, bailen o toquen, saben que no es posible ninguna emoción sin la llegada del duende. Ellos engañan a la gente y pueden dar sensación de duende sin haberla, como os engañan todos los días autores o pintores o modistos literarios sin duende, pero basta fijarse un poco y no dejarse llevar por la indiferencia, para descubrir la trampa y hacerles huir con su burdo artificio.

Una vez la cantaora andaluza Pastora Pavón, *la Niña de los Peines*, sombrío genio hispánico equivalente en capacidad de fantasía a Goya o Rafael el Gallo, cantaba en una tabernilla de Cádiz. Jugaba con su voz de sombra, con su voz de estaño fundido, con su voz cubierta de musgo; y se la enredaba en la cabellera o la mojaba en manzanilla o la perdía por unos jarales obscuros y lejanísimos. Pero nada; era inútil. Los oyentes permanecían callados.

Allí estaba Ignacio Espeleta, hermoso como una tortuga romana, a quien preguntaron una vez: «¿Cómo no trabajas?», y él, con una sonrisa digna de Argantonio, respondió: «¿Cómo voy a trabajar si soy de Cádiz?». Allí estaba Elvira la Caliente, aristócrata ramera de Sevilla, descendiente directa de Soledad Vargas, que en el 30 no se quiso casar con un Rothschild porque no la igualaba en sangre. Allí estaban los Guarriros, que la gente cree carniceros, pero en realidad son sacerdotes milenarios que siguen sacrificando toros a Gerión. Y en un ángulo el imponente ganadero don Pablo Murube con un aire de máscara cretense. Pastora Pavón terminó de cantar en medio del silencio. Solo y con sarcasmo un hombre pequeñito, de esos hombrines bailarines que salen de pronto de las botellas de aguardiente, dijo en voz muy baja: «¡Viva París!», como diciendo: «Aquí no nos importan las facultades, ni la técnica ni la maestría. Nos importa otra cosa».

Entonces la Niña de los Peines se levantó como una loca, tronchada igual que una llorona medieval, y se bebió de un trago un gran vaso de cazalla como fuego y se sentó a cantar, sin voz, sin aliento, sin matices, con la garganta abrasada, pero... con duende. Había logrado matar todo el andamiaje de la canción, para dejar paso a un duende furioso y avasallador, amigo de los vientos cargados de arena, que hacía que los oyentes se rasgaran los trajes, casi con el mismo ritmo con que se los rompen los negros antillanos del rito lucumí apelotonados ante la imagen de Santa Bárbara.

La Niña de los Peines tuvo que desgarrar su voz, porque sabía que la estaba oyendo gente exquisita que no pedía formas sino tuétano de forma, música pura con el cuerpo sucinto para poderse mantener en el aire. Se tuvo que empobrecer de facultades y de seguridades, es decir, tuvo que alejar a su musa y quedarse desamparada, que su duende viniera y se dignara luchar a brazo partido. ¡Y cómo cantó! Su voz ya no jugaba, su voz era un chorro de sangre digna, por su dolor y su sinceridad, de abrirse como una mano de diez dedos por los pies clavados, pero llenos de borrasca, de un Cristo de Juan de Juni.

La llegada del duende presupone siempre un cambio radical en todas las formas. Sobre planos viejos, da sensaciones de frescura totalmente inéditas, con una calidad de cosa recién creada, de milagro, que llega a producir un entusiasmo casi religioso.

En toda la música árabe, danza, canción o elegía, la llegada del duende es saludada con enérgicos «¡Alá, Alá!», «¡Dios, Dios!», tan cerca del «¡Olé!» de los toros que quién sabe si será lo mismo, y en todos los cantos del sur de España la aparición del duende es seguida por sinceros gritos de «¡Viva Dios!», profundo, humano, tierno grito de una comunicación con Dios por medio de los cinco sentidos gracias al duende que agita la voz y el cuerpo de la bailarina; evasión real y poética de este mundo, tan pura como la conseguida por el rarísimo poeta del XVII Pedro Soto de Rojas a través de siete jardines, o la de Juan Clímaco por una temblorosa escala de llanto.

Naturalmente, cuando esta evasión está lograda todos sienten sus efectos; el iniciado, viendo cómo el estilo vence a una materia pobre, y el ignorante, en el no sé qué de una auténtica emoción. Hace años, en un concurso de baile de Jerez de la Frontera se llevó el premio una vieja de ochenta años contra hermosas mujeres y muchachos con la cintura de agua, por el solo hecho de levantar los brazos, erguir la cabeza y dar un golpe con el pie sobre el tabladillo; pero en la reunión de musas y de ángeles que había allí, belleza de forma y belleza de sonrisa, tenía que ganar y ganó aquel duende moribundo, que arrastraba sus alas de cuchillos oxidados por el suelo.

Todas las artes son capaces de duende, pero donde encuentra más campo, como es natural, es en la música, en la danza y en la poesía hablada, ya que estas necesitan un cuerpo vivo que interprete, porque son formas que nacen y mueren de modo perpetuo y alzan sus contornos sobre un presente exacto. Muchas veces el duende del músico pasa al duende del intérprete, y otras veces, cuando el músico o el poeta no son tales, el duende del intérprete, y esto es interesante, crea una nueva maravilla que tiene en la apariencia, nada más, la forma primitiva. Tal, el caso de la enduendada Eleonora Duse, que buscaba obras fracasadas para hacerlas triunfar gracias a lo que ella inventaba, o el caso de Paganini, explicado por Goethe, que hacía oír melodías profundas de verdaderas vulgaridades, o el caso de una deliciosa muchacha del Puerto de Santa María a quien yo le vi cantar y bailar el horroroso cuplé italiano «¡Oh Mari!» con unos ritmos, unos silencios y una intención que hacían de la pacotilla napolitana una dura serpiente de oro levantado. Lo que pasa es que, efectivamente, encontraban alguna cosa nueva que nada tenía que ver con lo anterior, que ponían sangre viva y ciencia sobre cuerpos vacíos de expresión.

Todas las artes, y aun los países, tienen capacidad de duende, de ángel y de musa. Y así como Alemania tiene, con excepciones, musa, y la Italia tiene permanentemente ángel, España está en todos tiempos movida por el duende. Como país de música y danzas milenarias donde el duende exprime limones de madrugada y como país de muerte. Como país abierto a la Muerte.

En todos los países la muerte es un fin. Llega y se corren las cortinas. En España no. En España se levantan. Muchas gentes viven allí entre muros, hasta el día en que mueren y las sacan al sol. Un muerto en España está más vivo como muerto que en ningún sitio del mundo: hiere su perfil como el filo de una navaja barbera. El chiste sobre la muerte o su contemplación silenciosa son familiares a los españoles. Desde *El sueño de las calaveras* de Quevedo hasta el *Obispo podrido* de Valdés Leal, y desde la Marbella del siglo XVII, muerta de parto en mitad del camino, que dice:

> La sangre de mis entrañas
> cubriendo el caballo está;
> las patas de tu caballo
> echan fuego de alquitrán,

al reciente mozo de Salamanca, muerto por el toro, que clama:

> Amigos, que yo me muero;
> amigos, yo estoy muy malo.
> Tres pañuelos tengo dentro
> y este que meto son cuatro

hay una barandilla de flores de salitre donde se asoma un pueblo de contempladores de la muerte; con versículo de Jeremías por el lado más áspero o con ciprés fragante por el lado más lírico, pero un país donde lo más importante de todo tiene un último valor metálico de muerte.

La casulla y la ventana y la rueda del carro y la navaja y las barbas pinchosas de los pastores y la luna pelada y la mosca y las alacenas húmedas y los derribos y los santos cubiertos de encaje y la cal y la línea hiriente de aleros y miradores, tienen en España diminutas hierbas de muerte, alusiones y voces perceptibles para un espíritu alerta, que nos llenan la memoria con el aire yerto de nuestro propio tránsito. No es casualidad todo el arte español ligado con nuestra tierra llena de cardos y piedras definitivas, no es un ejemplo aislado la lamentación de Pleberio o las danzas del maestro Josef María de Valdivielso, no es un azar el que en toda la balada europea se destaque esta amada española:

> Si tú eres mi linda amiga,
> ¿cómo no me miras, di?
> Ojos con que te miraba
> a la sombra se los di.
> Si tú eres mi linda amiga,
> ¿cómo no me besas, di?

Labios con que te besaba
a la tierra se los di.
Si tú eres mi linda amiga,
¿cómo no me abrazas, di?
Brazos con que te abrazaba
de gusanos los cubrí.

ni es extraño que en los albores de nuestra lírica suene esta canción:

Dentro del vergel
moriré.
Dentro del rosal
matar me han.
Yo me iba, mi madre,
las rosas coger,
hallara la muerte
dentro del vergel.
Yo me iba, mi madre,
las rosas cortar,
hallara la muerte
dentro del rosal.
Dentro del vergel
moriré,
dentro del rosal,
matar me han.

Las cabezas heladas por la luna que pintó Zurbarán, el amarillo manteca con el amarillo relámpago del Greco, el relato del Padre Sigüenza, la obra íntegra de Goya, el ábside de la iglesia del Escorial, toda la escultura policromada, la cripta de la casa ducal de Osuna, la muerte con la guitarra de la capilla de los Benavente en Medina de Rioseco, equivalen, en lo culto, a la romería de San Andrés de Teixido, donde los muertos llevan sitio en la procesión, a los cantos de difuntos que cantan las mujeres de Asturias con faroles llenos de llamas en la noche de noviembre, al canto y danza de la Sibila en las catedrales de Mallorca y Toledo, al obscuro *In recort* tortosino, y a los innumerables ritos del Viernes Santo que, con la cultísima Fiesta de los Toros, forman el triunfo popular de la muerte española. En el mundo solamente México puede cogerse de la mano con mi país.

Cuando la musa ve llegar a la muerte, cierra la puerta o levanta un plinto o pasea una urna, y escribe un epitafio con mano de cera, pero en seguida vuelve a regar su laurel con un silencio que vacila entre dos brisas. Bajo el arco truncado de la Oda, ella junta con sentido fúnebre las flores exactas que pintaron los italianos del XV y llama al seguro gallo de Lucrecio para que espante sombras imprevistas.

Cuando ve llegar a la muerte el ángel, vuela en círculos lentos y teje con lágrimas de hielo y narcisos la elegía que hemos visto temblar en las manos de Keats y en las de Villasandino y en las de Herrera, en las de Bécquer y en las de Juan Ramón Jiménez. Pero ¡qué terror el del ángel si siente una araña, por diminuta que sea, sobre su tierno pie rosado!

En cambio, el duende no llega si no ve posibilidad de muerte, si no sabe que ha de rondar su casa, si no tiene seguridad que ha de mecer esas ramas que todos llevamos, que no tienen, que no tendrán consuelo.

Con idea, con sonido o con gesto, el duende gusta de los bordes del pozo en franca lucha con el creador. Ángel y musa se escapan, con violín o compás, y el duende hiere y en la curación de esta herida que no se cierra nunca está lo insólito, lo inventado de la obra de un hombre.

La virtud mágica del poema consiste en estar siempre enduendado para bautizar con agua obscura a todos los que lo miran, porque con duende es más fácil amar, comprender, y es *seguro* ser amado, ser comprendido, y esta lucha por la expresión y por la comunicación de la expresión adquiere a veces en poesía caracteres mortales.

Recordad el caso de la flamenquísima y enduendada Santa Teresa, flamenca no por atar un toro furioso y darle tres magníficos pases, que lo hizo, ni por presumir de guapa delante de fray Juan de la Miseria, ni por darle una bofetada al Nuncio de Su Santidad, sino por ser una de las pocas criaturas cuyo duende (no cuyo ángel, porque el ángel no ataca nunca) la traspasa con un dardo queriendo matarla por haberle quitado su último secreto, el puente sutil que une los cinco sentidos con ese centro en carne viva, en nube viva, en mar viva, del Amor libertado del Tiempo.

Valentísima vencedora del duende y caso contrario al de Felipe de Austria, que, ansiando buscar musa y ángel en la teología y en la astronomía, se vio aprisionado por el duende de los ardores fríos, en esa obra del Escorial, donde la geometría limita con el sueño y donde el duende se pone careta de musa para eterno castigo del gran rey.

Hemos dicho que el duende ama el borde de la herida y se acerca a los sitios donde las formas se funden en un anhelo superior a sus expresiones visibles.

En España (como en los pueblos de Oriente donde la danza es expresión religiosa) tiene el duende un campo sin límites sobre los cuerpos de las bailarinas de Cádiz, elogiadas por Marcial, sobre los pechos de los que cantan, elogiados por Juvenal, y en toda la liturgia de los toros, auténtico drama religioso, donde, de la misma manera que en la misa, se adora y se sacrifica a un dios.

Parece como si todo el duende del mundo clásico se agolpara en esta fiesta perfecta, exponente de la cultura y la gran sensibilidad de un pueblo que descubre en el hombre sus mejores iras, sus mejores bilis y su mejor llanto. Ni en el baile español ni en los toros se divierte nadie; el duende se encarga de hacer sufrir, por medio del drama sobre formas vivas, y prepara las escaleras para una evasión de la realidad que circunda.

El duende opera sobre el cuerpo de la bailarina como el aire sobre la arena. Convierte con mágico poder una hermosa muchacha en paralítica de la luna, o llena de rubores adolescentes a un viejo roto que pide limosna por las tiendas de vino; da con una cabellera olor de puerto nocturno y en todo momento opera sobre los brazos, en expresiones que son madres de la danza de todos los tiempos.

Pero imposible repetirse nunca. Esto es muy interesante de subrayar. El duende no se repite como no se repiten las formas del mar en la borrasca.

En los toros, adquiere sus acentos más impresionantes porque tiene que luchar, por un lado, con la muerte que puede destruirlo y, por otro lado, con la geometría, con la medida, base fundamental de la fiesta.

El toro tiene su órbita, el torero la suya y entre órbita y órbita un punto de peligro, donde está el vértice del terrible juego.

Se puede tener musa con la muleta y ángel con las banderillas y pasar por buen torero, pero en la faena de capa, con el toro limpio todavía de heridas, y en el momento de matar, se necesita la ayuda del duende para dar en el clavo de la verdad artística.

El torero que asusta al público en la plaza con su temeridad no torea, sino que está en ese plano ridículo, al alcance de cualquier hombre, de *jugarse la vida*; en cambio, el torero mordido por el duende da una lección de música pitagórica y hace olvidar que tira constantemente el corazón sobre los cuernos.

Lagartijo con su duende romano, Joselito con su duende judío, Belmonte con su duende barroco y Cagancho con su duende gitano enseñan desde el crepúsculo del anillo a poetas, pintores y músicos, cuatro grandes caminos de la tradición española.

España es el único país donde la muerte es el espectáculo nacional, donde la muerte toca largos clarines a la llegada de las primaveras, y su arte está siempre regido por un duende agudo que le ha dado su diferencia y su cualidad de invención.

El duende que llena de sangre, por vez primera en la escultura, las mejillas de los santos del maestro Mateo de Compostela, es el mismo que hace gemir a San Juan de la Cruz o quema ninfas desnudas por los sonetos religiosos de Lope.

El duende que levanta la torre de Sahagún o trabaja calientes ladrillos en Calatayud o Teruel, es el mismo que rompe las nubes del Greco y echa a volar a puntapiés alguaciles de Quevedo y quimeras de Goya.

Cuando llueve, saca a Velázquez enduendado en secreto detrás de sus grises monárquicos; cuando nieva, hace salir a Herrera desnudo para demostrar que el frío no mata; cuando arde, mete en sus llamas a Berruguete y le hace inventar un nuevo espacio para la escultura.

La musa de Góngora y el ángel de Garcilaso han de soltar la guirnalda de laurel cuando pasa el duende de San Juan de la Cruz, cuando

el ciervo vulnerado
por el otero asoma.

La musa de Gonzalo de Berceo y el ángel del Arcipreste de Hita se han de apartar para dejar paso a Jorge Manrique cuando llega herido de muerte a las puertas del Castillo de Belmonte. La musa de Gregorio Hernández y el ángel de José de Mora han de alejarse para que cruce el duende que llora lágrimas de sangre de Mena, y el duende con cabeza de toro asirio de Martínez Montañés; como la melancólica musa de Cataluña y el ángel mojado de Galicia han de mirar con amoroso asombro al duende de Castilla, tan lejos del pan caliente y de la dulcísima vaca, que pasa con normas de cielo barrido y tierra seca.

Duende de Quevedo y duende de Cervantes, con verdes anémonas de fósforo el uno y flores de yeso de Ruidera el otro, coronan el retablo del duende de España.

Cada arte tiene, como es natural, un duende de modo y forma distinta, pero todos uncen sus raíces en un punto, de donde manan los sonidos negros de Manuel Torres, materia última y fondo común incontrolable y estremecido, de leño, son, tela y vocablo.

Sonidos negros detrás de los cuales están ya en tierna intimidad los volcanes, las hormigas, los céfiros y la gran noche apretándose la cintura con la Vía Láctea.

Señoras y señores: He levantado tres arcos y con mano torpe he puesto en ellos a la musa, al ángel y al duende.

La musa permanece quieta; puede tener la túnica de pequeños pliegues, o los ojos de vaca que miran en Pompeya o la narizota de cuatro caras con que su gran amigo Picasso la ha pintado. El ángel puede agitar cabellos de Antonello de Messina, túnica de Lippi y violín de Masolino o de Rousseau.

El duende... ¿Dónde está el duende? Por el arco vacío entra un aire mental que sopla con insistencia sobre las cabezas de los muertos, en busca de nuevos paisajes y acentos ignorados; un aire con olor de saliva de niño, de hierba machacada y velo de medusa que anuncia el constante bautizo de las cosas recién creadas.

IMAGINATION, INSPIRATION, EVASION

5. Lorca at Marianao Beach at Havana, Cuba, 1930, the year he read "Imagination, Inspiration, Evasion." Lorca's friend the musicologist Adolfo Salazar wrote of his—and the poet's—fascination with the music and food they found every night in the "kiosks" of the Marianao neighborhood, the popular answer to elegant nightclubs of Havana. Photograph from Federico García Lorca Papers, Cuban Heritage Collection, University of Miami Library.

IN AN INTIMATE GATHERING AT THE RESIDENCIA DE ESTUDIANTES,[1] the architect Le Corbusier once said that what he had best liked about Spain was the expression *dar la estocada*, to make a clean kill, because it expressed a determination to get directly to the subject at hand and the desire to master it rapidly, without pausing over the merely accessory and decorative. [2]

I too believe in the doctrine of the *estocada*, although, naturally, I'm not exactly the most elegant or agile of matadors. The bull—the theme—is before us, and we must kill it. Grant me, at least, my good intentions.[3]

Imagination, inspiration, and evasion: the three degrees, the three steps sought and taken by any true work of art, by all literary history, and any poet conscious of the treasure God has given him.[4]

I know perfectly well how difficult this subject is, and I am not trying to define, only to emphasize. I don't want to delineate, I want to suggest. The mission of the poet is just that—*animar*, in the exact sense of the word: to give soul.[5] But don't ask me about truth or falsehood, because the meaning of "poetic truth" changes from one person to another. Light in Dante can be ugliness in Mallarmé. Furthermore, as everyone knows by now, poetry must be received rather than understood; loved, not analyzed.[6] No one should say "this is clear," because poetry is obscure. And no one should say "this is obscure," because poetry is clear. What we must do is search out poetry energetically and virtuously so that she will give herself to us. We need to have forgotten poetry completely before she can fall naked into our arms. The poet as watchman and the people. What poetry cannot bear is indifference, the devil's armchair. But it is indifference we hear babbling in the streets, dressed grotesquely in self-satisfaction and culture.

For me, imagination is synonymous with aptitude for discovery. To imagine, to discover, to carry our spotlight to the living penumbra where all the infinite possibilities, forms and numbers exist.

I do not believe in creation but in discovery, and I don't believe in the artist who stays in his seat, but in the one who walks the road. The imagination is a spiritual apparatus, a luminous explorer of the world, and it discovers, sketches, and gives clear life to fragments of the invisible reality where man is stirring.

The daughter of the imagination—the logical and legitimate daughter—is the metaphor, which is sometimes born from a sudden stroke of intuition or brought to light by the slow anguish of presentiment.

But the imagination is limited by reality: one cannot imagine what does not exist. It needs objects, landscapes, numbers, planets, and it requires the purest sort of logic to relate these things to one another. One cannot leap into the abyss or do away altogether with the terms of reality. Imagination has its horizons, it wants to delineate and solidify all that lies within its reach.

The poetic imagination travels and transforms things, giving them their purest meaning, their characteristic cut and contour, and points out and defines unsuspected relations, but it always *always* works upon the facts and forms of a clear, precise reality. Everything brought to us by the imagination fits nicely in our houses, within our human logic, controlled by reason, from which it can never break free.

The imagination hovers over reason like fragrance over a flower, without freeing itself from its petals, following the movements of the breeze but tied, always, to the ineffable center of its origin.

In no way can imagination remain alone in the void or create relations where they do not already exist. This would be contrary to its nature and its basic foundation: the five bodily senses.

To come alive, it needs proportions, masses, distances, logical expression. When it tries to embrace too much, when it imagines it has the three hundred wings of a seraph, it falls into monstrosity, into ruin and ugliness, or smashes its head against the wall.

Its special mechanism of creation requires order and limits. It was imagination that invented the four cardinal directions and discovered the intermediate causes of things and gave names, but imagination has never been able to abandon its hands in the burning embers, without logic or meaning, where inspiration is stirring, unchained and free.

So then, the imagination is the first step and the foundation of all poetry, the cool, green, field draped in moonlight where the transparent airships of free, inhuman inspiration—insect wings and planetary nickel—are sleeping.

The mechanics of poetic imagination are always the same: a concentration, a leap, a flight, the hunt for imagery, a return with the treasure, and a classification and selection of what has been brought back.[7] The poet commands his imagination and takes it wherever he wants to. When he is not happy with its services, he punishes it and sends it out again, just as the hunter punishes the dog too slow in bringing him the prey.[8]

With his imagination the poet builds a tower against the elements and against mystery.[9] He is unassailable. He orders and is obeyed. But the best, most resplendent birds always get away from him.

It is difficult for a "purely imaginative" poet (so to speak) to produce intense emotions with his poetry, which is wholly the product of reason.[10] Poetic emotions, surely not. He *can*, of course, use his verse technique and verbal mastery to produce that musical emotion typical of the Romantics, which almost always falls short of the deep spiritual meaning of the pure poem. But in no way can the imaginative poet produce virginal, unrestrained poetic emotion, emotion without walls—perfectly complete poetry with laws newly created just for her[11] and for her unknown sky.

The imagination is poor, and the poetic imagination even more so. Visible reality, the facts of the world and of the human body have much more subtle nuance and are much more poetic than anything imagination can discover.

We often see this in the struggle between scientific reality and imaginative myth, in which—thank God—science proves itself a thousand times more lyrical than any theogony.[12]

The human imagination has invented giants in order to explain the construction of great grottos or enchanted cities. Later, reality taught us that those great caves and enchanted cities are made by water drops.[13] The pure, patient, eternal drop of water. In this case, as in many others, reality wins. And the instinct of the water drop is more beautiful than the hand of a giant. In poetry, the truth of reality trumps imagination, which discovers its own poverty. Imagination was about to attribute to giants what logically seemed the work of giants. But scientific reality, which is poetical in extreme and transcends the realm of logic, restored their truth to the pure, perennial drops of water. And it is, after all, much more beautiful that a cave be a mysterious caprice of the water—enchained and ordered by eternal laws—than the whim of giants whose only meaning is to provide an explanation.

The imagination, though we may believe the opposite, has relatively little room to operate, has too stiff a backbone, and is always defeated by the beauty of visible reality.

And it always loses. The ancient nymphs who called out to old sailors of rivers in order to take out their hearts (an imaginative myth) have been replaced by the echo, a geometric mystery more impressive in its ultimate plastic essence, than the voices of those cruel female swimmers.[14] The discovery of the eclipse cooled the overheated imagination that clouded the spotless blue with human breath. The forests of red flowers and violent perfumes that man once placed among the stars were swept away by this formula for astronomical hygiene. A theorem of light and shadow destroys the anguish-ridden ambit of conjecture.[15]

So then, the imagination is always, sooner or later, conquered by the reality she herself discovers.

The poet strolls back and forth through his imagination, enclosed by it.

But he isn't happy there. He knows that his imaginative sense can be trained; that it can be enriched through a sort of gymnastics; that he can teach it to lengthen its sight waves and antennae of light. But the poet is sadly frustrated—wanting but not being able—in his inner landscape.

He hears the great rivers flowing silently by, without anyone listening to their music. To his brow comes the coolness of reeds that tremble in Never-Never Land. He wants to hear the dialogue of the insects in the slimy moss beneath incredible boughs tied by strings of light to the exact half-moon.

He wants to penetrate the current of the sap in the dark, fast silence of the great tree trunks.

He wants to understand the Morse code spoken by the heart of the sleeping girl.

He wants, he wants. We all *want*. He wants, but he cannot. He pounds on the walls of the imagination and gets nowhere. He turns and tries to fly, but it is all useless.

If he makes the insects speak—the insects in the moss under those incredible boughs—he will give their dialogue human words and feelings, but not the feelings of insects, because the imagination can never plumb those depths.[16]

If he wants to express the almost mental music of the sap rising and falling in the dark, fast silence of those great tree trunks, he will invent a music related to something he has seen and heard, something with a certain "plastic" resemblance: he'll come up with the image of a water jet, for example, or he will turn the sap in the dark, fast silence of those great tree trunks into a dream of distant waterjets, a melody of pulsing veins, but without capturing the sap's impossibly exact tenderness, the peculiar murmur of that unimaginable liquid. The poet wants. He wants but can't. And that is precisely his sin: to *want*.[17]

As long as he doesn't try to free himself from the world, the poet can live happily in his golden poverty. All the rhetorical systems, all the poetic schools in the world, from the schematics of the Japanese to the graceful steed of French poetry or the golden column of Andalucía, have a closet of lovely props: suns, moons, lilies, mirrors, and melancholy clouds for the use of every intelligence and latitude.

But for the poet who wants to break free from the World, his enemy,[18] the ambit of his imagination becomes unbearable. To live at the expense of the image is quite sad, and to live off the poetry produced by objects of reality leads to ennui. And so, the poet stops imagining. He stops daydreaming and stops wanting things. He no longer wants. We all want, but he does not. He loves. He loves. He loves and he *can*. He goes from wanting to love. And he who loves does not want. He leaves imagination, which is a fact of the soul, and takes the path of inspiration, which is a state of the soul. He goes from analysis to faith.

The poet, who was once an explorer, is now a humble person who feels on his back the irresistible beauty of all things. Here there are no terms or limits, no explicable laws, only an admirable freedom!

Just as the poetic imagination has a human logic, poetic inspiration has a poetic logic.[19]

Here things exist *just because*, with no explicable cause or effect. Inspiration is a state of faith in the midst of the most absolute humility. Acquired poetic technique is no longer of any use, and it cannot follow any aesthetic postulates. And just as the imagination is discovery, inspiration is a boon, an ineffable gift. We are now up over the rooftops, in the open air, without walls or limits, in the realm of free, beautiful, dethroned poetry.[20] No explanation is possible. The newly captured prey is safe from the sure, clumsy, crab claws of analysis.[21] We no longer have to knit our brow or separate one element from another in order to understand. Emotion comes to us noble and direct, as unrepeatable as the sudden breeze that tenderly ruffles this or that corner of the morning.

But a poem is almost never, at all moments, totally inspired. It has its points of light and its strong gusts of wind. We ought to be content and even happy about that. But this is difficult. Inspiration has a formidable enemy, which is the imagination and its capacity for equilibrium. It is also attacked by physics, mathematics, almost all the sciences, and the self-assured person who doesn't want to wound worldly laws. I'm talking here about pure inspiration, the inspiration that has no name and that trembles like a virgin before the self-satisfied mask of irony, age-old irony, steeped in the sins of the world, which mocks the poetic innocence that appears before it naked, refusing to justify itself.[22] "This, that comes to me in the quality of innocence," Larrea says in one of his poems.[23]

There are certain mechanisms for hunting for inspiration—baits and bright lures to make it come to us. But this takes some really difficult training and a huge amount of work. One must have complete faith in poetry, an almost perfect state of material and spiritual virtue, and must know how to vehemently reject any temptation to be understood. Inspiration often attacks intelligence head-on, assaulting the natural order of things. One must look through the eyes of a child and ask for the moon; ask for the moon and believe they can put it in our hands.

Imagination attacks a theme furiously from all angles, but inspiration receives it suddenly and wraps it in subtle, pulsing light, like those huge carnivorous flowers that envelop the trembling bee and dissolve it in the acrid juice exuded by their merciless petals.

Imagination is intelligent, orderly, full of balance, but inspiration is sometimes incongruous and inhuman, and puts a livid worm in the clear blue eyes of our muse. Just because it *wants* to, without our being able to understand. Imagination creates a poetic ambience, and inspiration invents the "poetic fact" or event. The imagination creates the theorem, and inspiration, the miracle.[24] Obviously, when I speak of the poet, I'm referring to the real thing, and unfortunately, such creatures are rare. There are very few poets, and poetry doesn't often give herself to them. I would be satisfied if even once, over an entire lifetime, I could make unscathed, naked poetry sing in her silver voice.

We are approaching the very pith of poetry, the advent of the "poetic fact" discovered by inspiration.

A fact with its own life, its own laws, which breaks with any logical control or intelligent light.[25]

Poetry in itself! Full of an order and a harmony exclusively poetic. The poem that has evaded imaginative reality is no longer subject to the criteria of ugly or beautiful (as they are now understood) and it enters an amazing poetic reality which is sometimes full of tenderness and sometimes full of penetrating cruelty.[26]

[The lecturer] went on a rapid excursion through the miracles described by Jacobus de Voragine in The Golden Legend, *and described the legend of Saint Bridget, whose virginal fingers populated the wood of the altar with vivid echoes, flowering branches, and birds nests. The miracle is a form of pure emotion, beauty that cannot be explained. For additional examples he draws on his own* Gypsy Ballads.... *a book in which there are infinite, inexplicable, pure poetic facts, little noticed because they are in the line of imaginative poems [...]*

> Green, I want you green,
> Green wind, green boughs.

which has a strong traditional flavor.

> A thousand crystal tambourines
> were wounding the dawn

from "Dead of Love,"[27] and other examples, which are not so inexplicable in their inner coherence as he himself imagines.[28]

In the history of Spanish poetry are two great poets who represent the poetry of imagination and the poetry of inspiration: Luis de Góngora and Saint John of the Cross.

One cannot delimit these two realms with mathematical precision. In both, when they are true, we find the living air of poetry.[29]

With his verbal equilibrium and vivid, exact line, Góngora is the perfect imaginative poet. His inner horizons are pure stone, high noon. He doesn't want what lies beyond his reach. He has no mystery and is a stranger to insomnia. His poem approaches the expression of mathematics and pure formula, and lets life pass him by. Pure form, pure formula. Imagination and technique.

By contrast, San Juan de la Cruz is flight and yearning. Yearning for perspective and boundless love. His *Spiritual Canticle* is the most inspired book any literature could produce. What is ratiocination in Góngora is faith in John of the Cross. When Góngora is striking flint, John of the Cross is wounding himself.

To be sure, Góngora is the austere academician, the terrible professor of language and poetry. John of the Cross will always be the disciple of the elements, the man who grazes the mountaintops with the soles of his feet. The exaltation of Góngora which all of Spanish youth has felt, and in which I collaborated with great enthusiasm in my own clumsy way, [30] has coincided with the maturity of Cubism, a painting based on pure ratiocination, austere in color and arabesque, tied to immutable laws of plasticity: a breeze that blew from Raphael Sanzio and Mantegna and culminated in the austere theorems of color and arabesque of the ultra-Castilian Juan Gris.

The Cubist pays no attention to the gifts of inspiration. He has enough with geometry and arithmetic. He stylizes and suppresses and knows perfectly well that a rhythm traveling in one direction requires a rhythm traveling in the other, and he doesn't throw things off balance or get passionate about things he shouldn't. Cubism has taught art the greatest-ever lesson of discipline. The anatomy of a painting has been studied down to its very last detail. Dissection of the imagination. The splendid still lifes of Cézanne, where a worm could all too easily gnaw into his round apples, were autopsied by Juan Gris with his cold still lifes with their lunar beauty, within the purest kind of plastic abstraction.[31] This had to happen. Impressionism was turning into a trick, and one had to flee the mist and take refuge in the concrete. But what happens to us there? We bang our heads against the walls and fill our hearts with cold sunlight.

In our epoch all the arts are becoming poetic. All seek the pinprick, the living, perennial point of pure emotion. Emotion that is both carried away by the wind, yes, but is totally resistant to time.

In general, painters and poets, after the pure breeze of Cubism, turn their eyes to pure instinct, to uncontrolled virginal creation, to the cool source of direct emotion, resting on the irrepressible strength of their own newly discovered souls.

He mentions the new values of Spanish poetry. Juan Larrea and his disciple Gerardo Diego use chains of poetic facts to construct their poems, which grow more and more limpid and acquire a more crystalline flight.[32]

On his own path, Rafael Alberti has taken his poetry to a difficult beautiful summit, infusing it with an eternal air. On the opposite bank, the prodigious magician Jorge Guillén breathes into his poetry the phosphorescent, the mysterious, and the Machiavellian, and Pedro Salinas, modest and enlightened, abandons his poems in an uninhabited living room, where his carefully hidden footsteps—those of a master—glisten in the dust. This school is a renaissance, a "return to nature" in reaction to the academicisms of the mature period of cubism.[33]

Plastic expression becomes poetic in order to take in vital juices and cleanse itself from the decorative ailments of the last of cubism...

[He says that] the latest generations of poets have tried to free poetry not only from anecdote but also from the riddle of the image, removing it from the plane of reality; in other words, take poetry to a higher level of purity and simplicity, to a different reality.[34] *They try to leap into a world of virgin emotions and imbue their poems with planetary feeling [...] Evasion of reality through dream, by way of the subconscious, by way of some unheard-of "fact" gifted to the poet by inspiration. [...] Surrealism uses the dream, the most real world of dreams, and there, without a doubt, one finds authentic poetic norms. But this evasion by means of the dream or the subconscious is, although very pure, not very diaphanous.*

We Spaniards want profiles and visible mystery. Form and sensualities. In the north Surrealism can take hold¬¬—for example, modern German art,—but Spain, with her history, defends us from the strong liquor of dream.

This is what I think—at present—of the poetry I am writing. When I say "at present" I mean today. Tomorrow, I don't know what I will think. Because I am a true poet, and will remain so until my death, I will never stop flagellating myself with the disciplines, knowing that someday my body must spurt blood that's green or yellow. Anything but remain seated in the window looking out on the same landscape. The light of any poet is contradiction. I haven't tried to convince anyone—that would be unworthy of poetry. Poetry doesn't need skilled practitioners, she needs lovers, and she lays down brambles and splinters of glass for the hands that search for her with love.[32]

IMAGINACIÓN, INSPIRACIÓN, EVASIÓN

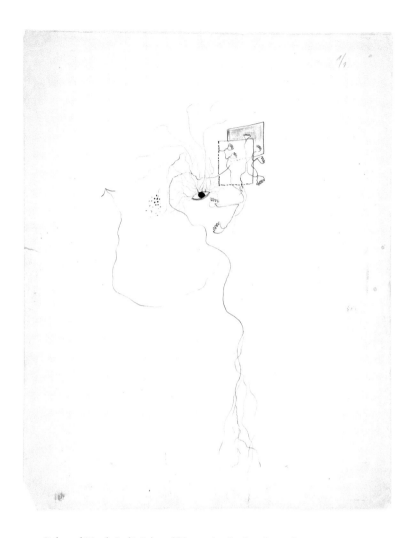

6. *Sight and Touch.* India ink and blue and red colored pencils on paper, ca. 1929-1930. In his essay on the seventeenth-century Spanish poet Góngora, his paragon of of he "imaginative" poet, Lorca writes that "A poet must be a professor of the five bodily senses, in this order: sight, touch, hearing, smell, and taste. And in order to master the most beautiful images, he must open doors between all of them" (*DS* 64). In "Duende: Play and Theory," the duende's most precious secret is "the subtle bridge between the five senses and the center of raw, live flesh, cloud or sea of Love freed from Time: (p. 31). Jean Gebser Series, Centro Federico García Lorca.

DIJO EL ARQUITECTO CORBUSIER EN UNA REUNIÓN ÍNTIMA DE LA Residencia de Estudiantes que lo que más le había gustado de España era la frase de «dar la estocada», porque expresaba la intención profunda de ir al tema y el ansia de dominarlo rápidamente, sin detenerse en lo accesorio y decorativo.

Yo también soy partidario de esta posición de la estocada, aunque naturalmente, no sea un espada de limpia agilidad. El toro (el tema) está delante y hay que matarlo. Valga siquiera mi buena intención.

Imaginación, inspiración, evasión: los tres grados, las tres etapas que busca y recorre toda obra de arte verdadera, toda la historia literaria, y todo poeta consciente del tesoro que maneja por la gracia de Dios.

Sé perfectamente las dificultades que este tema tiene, y no pretendo, por tanto, definir, sino subrayar; no quiero dibujar, sino sugerir. La misión del poeta es esta: animar, en su exacto sentido, dar alma. Pero no me preguntéis por lo verdadero y lo falso, porque la «verdad poética» es una expresión que cambia al mudar su enunciado. Lo que es luz en el Dante puede ser fealdad en Mallarmé. Y desde luego, ya es sabido por todo el mundo que la poesía no se entiende; la poesía se recibe. La poesía no se analiza; la poesía se ama. Nadie diga «esto es claro», porque la poesía es oscura; nadie diga que esto es oscuro, porque la poesía es clara. Es decir, necesitamos buscar, con esfuerzo y virtud, a la poesía para que esta se nos entregue. Necesitamos haber olvidado por completo la poesía para que esta caiga desnuda en nuestros brazos. El vigía poético y el pueblo. Lo que no admite de ningún modo la poesía es la indiferencia. La indiferencia es el sillón del demonio, pero ella es la que habla en las calles con un grotesco vestido de suficiencia y cultura.

Para mí la imaginación es sinónima de aptitud para el descubrimiento. Imaginar es descubrir, llevar nuestro foco de luz a la penumbra viva donde existen todas las infinitas posibilidades, formas y números.

No creo en la creación, sino en el descubrimiento, como no creo en el artista sentado, sino en el artista caminante. La imaginación es un aparato espiritual, un explorador luminoso del mundo, que descubre, dibuja y da vida clara a fragmentos de la realidad invisible donde se mueve el hombre.

La hija directa de la imaginación es la metáfora, hija legítima y lógica, nacida muchas veces con el golpe rápido de la intuición, o con la lenta angustia del presentimiento.

Pero la imaginación está limitada por la realidad: no se puede imaginar lo que no existe de ninguna manera. Necesita de objetos, paisajes, números, planetas, y se hacen precisas las relaciones entre ellos dentro de la lógica más pura. No se puede saltar al abismo ni prescindir de los términos reales. La imaginación tiene horizontes, quiere dibujar y concretar todo lo que abarca.

La imaginación poética viaja y transforma las cosas, les da su sentido más puro, su bisel más característico; define y señala relaciones que no se sospechaban, pero siempre siempre opera sobre hechos o formas de la realidad más neta y precisa. Todo lo que la imaginación nos trae lo podemos albergar en nuestra casa. Está dentro de nuestra lógica humana, está controlada por la razón, de la que nunca se desprende.

Vuela la imaginación sobre la razón como el perfume de la flor sobre la flor misma, sin desprenderse de los pétalos, siguiendo los movimientos de la brisa, pero apoyada siempre en el centro inefable de su origen.

No puede de ninguna manera la imaginación permanecer aislada en el vacío ni crear relaciones donde no las hay. Esto repugna a su naturaleza y a su base fundamental, que son los cinco sentidos corporales.

Necesita de proporciones, de masas, de distancias, y necesita de la expresión lógica para estar viva. Cuando quiere abarcar demasiado, cuando se figura que tiene las trescientas alas de un serafín, cae en lo monstruoso, en la fealdad deshecha, o se rompe la cabeza contra las paredes.

Su manera especial de crear, su mecanismo, necesita del orden y del límite. La imaginación es la que ha inventado los cuatro puntos cardinales, la que ha descubierto las causas intermedias de las cosas, la que ha puesto nombres, pero no ha podido nunca abandonar sus manos en las ascuas sin lógica ni sentido donde se mueve la inspiración, libre y sin cadenas.

Es la imaginación, pues, el primer escalón y la base de toda poesía, el campo de verdor enlunado donde duermen a veces los aviones transparentes—ala de insecto y níquel planetario—de la inspiración libertada e inhumana.

La mecánica de la imaginación poética es la misma en todos los momentos. Una concentración, un salto, un vuelo, una cacería de imágenes, una vuelta con el tesoro y una clasificación y selección de lo traído. El poeta domina a su imaginación, la lleva donde quiere y, no contento con sus servicios, la castiga y la vuelve a enviar, como el cazador al perro tardo en conseguir la pieza.

El poeta con su imaginación construye una torre contra los elementos y contra el misterio. Es inatacable, ordena y es escuchado. Pero se le escapan casi siempre las mejores aves y las más refulgentes luces.

Es difícil que un poeta imaginativo puro (llamémosle así) produzca emociones intensas con su poesía, razonada toda ella. Emociones poéticas, desde luego que no. Puede producir con la técnica del verso y la maestría verbal esa típica emoción musical de los románticos, desligada casi siempre del sentido espiritual y hondo del poema puro. Pero una emoción poética virgen, desligada e incontrolada, libre de paredes, poesía redonda con sus leyes recién creadas para ella y su cielo inédito, desde luego que no.

La imaginación es pobre, y la imaginación poética mucho más. La realidad visible, los hechos del mundo y del cuerpo humano son mucho más llenos de matices, son más poéticos que lo que ella descubre.

Esto se nota muchas veces en la lucha entablada entre la realidad científica y el mito imaginativo, en la cual vence, gracias a Dios, la ciencia, mucho más lírica mil veces que las teogonías.

La imaginación de los hombres ha inventado los gigantes para achacarles la construcción de las grandes grutas o ciudades encantadas. La realidad ha enseñado después que estas grandes grutas y ciudades encantadas están hechas por la gota de agua. Por la pura gota de agua, paciente y eterna. En este caso, como en otros muchos, la realidad ha vencido a la imaginación. Es más bello el instinto de la gota de agua que la mano del gigante. La verdad real vence a la imaginación en poesía, o sea, la imaginación misma descubre su pobreza. La imaginación estaba en el punto lógico de achacar a gigantes lo que parecía obra de gigantes; pero la realidad científica, poética en extremo y fuera del ámbito lógico, ponía en las gotas limpias del agua perenne su verdad. Porque es mucho mas bello que una gruta sea un misterioso capricho del agua, ordenada y encadenada a leyes eternas, que un capricho de unos gigantes que no tienen más sentido que el de una explicación.

La imaginación, aunque creamos lo contrario, tiene poco campo de acción relativamente; es demasiado vertebrada y está vencida en todo momento por la bella realidad visible.

Y siempre pierde. Las antiguas ninfas que llamaban a los viejos navegantes fluviales para quitarles el corazón (mito imaginativo) han sido sustituidas por el eco, misterio geométrico más impresionante en su última esencia plástica, que las voces de las crueles nadadoras. El descubrimiento de los eclipses acalló la imaginación calenturienta que ponía su aliento humano en el celeste impecable. Los bosques de flores rojas y violentos perfumes que el hombre ponía entre las estrellas fueron barridos con esta fórmula de higiene astronómica. Un teorema de luz y sombra destruye el ámbito angustioso de la conjetura.

La imaginación, pues, está siempre, más tarde o más temprano, vencida por la realidad que ella misma descubre.

El poeta pasea siempre por su imaginación; encerrado en su imaginación, va y viene.

Pero no se encuentra a gusto. Sabe que su sentido imaginativo es capaz de entrenamiento, sabe que existe una gimnasia de la imaginación, mediante la cual puede enriquecerla, enseñarla a agrandar sus antenas de luz y su onda emisora. Pero el poeta está en un triste quiero y no puedo, a solas con su paisaje interior.

Oye el fluir de grandes ríos que pasan en silencio, sin que nadie escuche su música. Hasta su frente llega la frescura que mana de los juncos que se mecen «en ninguna parte» Quiere sentir el diálogo de los insectos que se agitan en el musgo baboso, bajo las ramas increíbles, relacionadas directamente por cuerdas de luz con la exacta media luna.

Quiere penetrar la música de la corriente de la savia en el silencio oscuro y clavado de los grandes troncos.

Quiere comprender, apoyando su oído, el alfabeto morse que habla el corazón de la muchacha dormida.

Quiere, quiere. Todos queremos. Quiere, pero no puede. Golpea las paredes de su imaginación, gira y pretende vuelos, pero todo será inútil.

Si hace hablar a los insectos que se agitan en el musgo bajo las ramas increíbles, pondrá sentimientos y palabras humanas en sus discursos; pero no sentimientos de insecto, porque la imaginación no llega a esas profundidades jamás.

Si quiere expresar la música casi mental de la savia ascendente y descendente en el silencio oscuro y clavado de los grandes troncos, hará una música relacionada con algo que ha oído y visto, parecido «plásticamente» al fenómeno. Pondrá, por ejemplo, una imagen del surtidor. Hará de la savia en el silencio oscuro y clavado de los grandes troncos un sueño de surtidores lejanos, una melodía de venas palpitantes, pero sin la expresión justa e imposible de la ternura del líquido, [su] rumor concreto, ya fuera del ámbito imaginativo. El poeta quiere. Quiere y no puede. Este es su pecado. Querer.

Mientras no pretenda libertar[se] del mundo, puede el poeta vivir bien en su pobreza dorada. Las retóricas y todas las escuelas poéticas del universo, desde los esquemas japoneses, el agilísimo caballo de Francia o la columna dorada de Andalucía, tienen una hermosa guardarropía de soles, lunas, lirios, espejos y nubes melancólicas para uso de todas las inteligencias y latitudes.

Pero para el poeta que quiera libertarse del Mundo enemigo, ya su campo imaginativo le es insoportable. Vivir a costa de la imaginación es bien triste, por cierto. Vivir a costa de la poesía que producen los objetos reales, le causa cansancio. Entonces el poeta deja de imaginar. Deja de soñar despierto y deja de querer. Ya no quiere. Todos queremos. Pero él no quiere. Él ama. Ama y puede. Va del querer al amor. Y el que ama no quiere.

Pasa de la imaginación, que es un hecho del alma, al camino de la inspiración, que es un estado de alma. Pasa del análisis a la fe. De la imaginación a la inspiración.

El poeta, que era antes un explorador, ya es un hombre humilde, un hombre que siente sobre su espalda la irresistible belleza de todas las cosas. Ya no hay términos. Ya no hay límites. Ya no hay leyes explicadas. ¡Admirable libertad!

Así como la imaginación poética tiene una lógica humana, la inspiración poética tiene una lógica poética.

Ya las cosas son porque sí, sin que haya causa ni efecto explicable. La inspiración es un estado de fe en medio de la humildad más absoluta. La técnica poética adquirida ya no sirve, como no sirve ningún postulado estético sobre el que operar; y así como la imaginación es un descubrimiento, la inspiración es un don, un inefable regalo. Ya estamos sobre los tejados, al aire libre, sin paredes ni límites, en el estadio de la libre, de la bella, de la destronada poesía. Ya no cabe explicación alguna, ni el análisis puede meter sus pinzas de cangrejo, torpes y seguras, en la presa recién capturada. Ya no hay que arrugar el entrecejo ni separar los elementos para comprender. La emoción llega noble y directa, irreplicable, como la brisa repentina que ondula tiernamente algunos rincones de la mañana.

Lo que pasa es que el poema no es casi nunca inspirado en todos sus momentos. Tiene puntos de luz y a veces ráfagas intensas, pero ya basta con esto, y con esto nos debíamos contentar. Pero es difícil. La inspiración tiene un inmenso enemigo, que es la imaginación y su capacidad de equilibrio. Después la atacan la física, las matemáticas, casi todas las ciencias y el hombre seguro de sí mismo, que no quiere herir las leyes del mundo. Hablo de la inspiración pura, de la inspiración que no tiene nombre, de la que tiembla virginalmente ante la careta satisfecha de la ironía, la ironía vieja y requetevieja, resabiada en los pecados del mundo, que se burla de la inocencia poética que se presenta desnuda y no quiere justificarse.

La inspiración tiene también su mecánica para ser cazada. Hay cebos y espejitos para que venga a nosotros, pero este entrenamiento es dificilísimo y lleno de trabajos. Se necesita una fe rotunda en la poesía, se necesita un estado de virtud material y espiritual de cierta perfección, y se necesita saber rechazar con vehemencia toda tentación de ser comprendido. La inspiración ataca de plano muchas veces a la inteligencia y al orden natural de las cosas. Hay que mirar con ojos de niño y pedir la luna. Hay que pedir la luna y creer que nos la pueden poner en las manos.

La imaginación ataca el tema furiosamente por todas partes, y la inspiración lo recibe de pronto y lo envuelve en luz súbita y palpitante, como esas grandes flores carnívoras que encierran a la abeja, trémula de miedo, y la disuelven en el agrio jugo que sudan sus pétalos inmisericordes.

La imaginación es inteligente, ordenada, llena de equilibrio. La inspiración es incongruente en ocasiones, no conoce al hombre, y pone muchas veces un gusano lívido en los ojos claros de nuestra musa. Porque quiere. Sin que lo podamos comprender. Porque le gusta. La imaginación lle[g]a y da un ambiente poético, y la inspiración inventa el hecho poético. La imaginación crea el teorema, y la inspiración, el milagro. No necesito decir que, cuando digo «poeta» me refiero a un poeta auténtico, por desgracia tan raro. Hay poquísimos poetas y a estos se les entrega pocas veces la poesía. Yo me daría por satisfecho si a través de toda mi vida hiciera sonar por una vez siquiera la garganta de plata de la poesía ilesa y desnuda.

Nos acercamos a la médula misma de la poesía. A la aparición del hecho poético que la inspiración descubre.

Hecho que tiene vida propia, leyes inéditas, y que rompe con todo control lógico y toda luz inteligente.

¡Poesía en sí misma! Llena de orden y de armonía, pero de un orden y una armonía exclusivamente poéticos. El poema evadido de la realidad imaginativa se sustrae a los dictados de feo y bello como se entiende ahora y entra en una asombrosa realidad poética, a veces llena de ternura y a veces de la crueldad más penetrante.

Hizo una rápida excursión por los milagros descritos por Jacobo de Vorágine en La leyenda dorada, *y describió la leyenda de Santa Brígida, bajo cuyos dedos virginales se poblaban de ecos vivos, de ramas floridas, y de nidos las maderas del altar. El milagro es una forma de la emoción pura, la belleza inexplicable. Como ejemplo de sus frases cita versos de su Romancero gitano, en donde hay infinidad de 'hechos poéticos' puros, inexplicables, a veces poco notados por estar en la línea de poemas imaginativos* [...]

> *Verde, que te quiero verde;*
> *verde viento, verdes ramas,*

que tiene un fuerte sabor popular;

> *mil panderos de cristal*
> *herían la madrugada,*

de «Muerto de amor», y otras imágenes no tan inexplicables en su relación interior como él mismo se figura.

En la historia de la poesía española aparecen los dos grandes poetas representativos de estas zonas, imaginativa e inspirada. Góngora y San Juan de la Cruz.

No se puede precisar, como es natural, de manera matemática, dónde empieza la una y termina la otra. En todas ellas, cuando son verdaderas, existe el aire vivo de la poesía.

Góngora es el perfecto imaginativo, el equilibrio verbal y el dibujo concreto. Sus horizontes íntimos son piedra pura y hora de mediodía. No quiere lo que no puede conseguir. No tiene misterio, ni conoce el insomnio. Cerca de la expresión matemática acaba su poema, y deja la vida pasar. Es pura forma y pura fórmula. Imaginación y técnica.

En cambio, San Juan de la Cruz es lo contrario. Vuelo y anhelo. Afán de perspectivas y amor desatado. Su *Cántico espiritual* es el libro más inspirado que puede existir en una literatura. Lo que en Góngora es raciocinio, en San Juan es fe; lo que en Góngora es ataque al pedernal, en San Juan es herida propia.

Lo que ya no cabe duda es que Góngora es el académico, el austero académico, el terrible profesor de lengua y poesía. San Juan de la Cruz será siempre el discípulo de los elementos, el hombre que roza los montes con los dedos de sus pies. Precisamente, la última exaltación de Góngora, hecha por toda la juventud española, y a la cual yo he cooperado desde mis medios torpes con todo entusiasmo, corresponde a la madurez de la época cubista, pintura del raciocinio puro, atada a leyes plásticas inmutables.

Venía el aire de Rafael Sanzio y el aire del Mantegna a los teoremas austeros de color y arabesco que han culminado en el castellanísimo Juan Gris.

El cubista no hace caso ninguno de lo que puede darle la inspiración. Con la geometría y la aritmética tiene bastante. Estiliza y suprime. Sabe perfectamente que a un ritmo en una dirección corresponde otro ritmo en dirección contraria, y no rompe equilibrios ni se apasiona por lo que no debe. El cubismo ha dado al arte la lección más grande de disciplina que ha tenido jamás. Se ha estudiado hasta el último rincón la anatomía de un cuadro. Imaginación diseccionada. A las espléndidas naturalezas muertas que pintó Cézanne, todavía fáciles para que un gusano mordiera sus redondas manzanas, les hizo la autopsia Juan Gris con sus naturalezas frías, de belleza lunar, dentro de la más pura abstracción plástica. Era necesario hacerlo. El impresionismo deviene en truco. Había que huir de las nieblas y refugiarse en lo concreto. Pero ya en lo concreto, ¿a dónde vamos por ahí? Vamos a rompernos la cabeza contra las paredes y a crearnos un frío corazón de sol.

En la época presente todas las artes se hacen poéticas. Buscan el punto inefable de la emoción pura. Es decir, el punto vivo y perenne. Emoción que se la lleva el viento. Sí, se la lleva el viento, pero es inexpugnable para el tiempo.

Pero en general pintores y poetas después de la brisa pura del cubismo vuelven los ojos al puro instinto, a la creación virginal incontrolada, a la fuente fresquísima de la emoción directa, descansando bajo la fuerza irrefrenable de sus propias almas descubierta.

Citó los nuevos valores de la poesía española. Juan Larrea y su discípulo Gerardo Diego construyen poemas a base de hechos poéticos encadenados, cada vez más limpios de imagen y de vuelo más cristalino.

Aparte de ellos, Rafael Alberti conduce su poesía a una cumbre bella y difícil, traspasada de aire eterno. Enfrente, en la otra orilla, el mágico prodigioso Jorge Guillén infunde a su palabra un aliento fosforescente, misterioso, maquiavélico en la poesía castellana, y el modestísimo iluminado Pedro Salinas abandona sus poemas en una sala familiar, deshabitada, donde brillan sobre el polvo sus recatadas huellas de maestro. Esta escuela es un renacimiento, una «vuelta a la naturaleza» en reacción a los academicismos de la época madura del cubismo…

La plástica se hace poética para tomar jugos vitales y limpiarse de las dolencias, ya decorativas, del último cubismo.

[Dice que] las últimas generaciones de poetas [...] pretenden liberar la poesía no solo de la anécdota, sino del acertijo de la imagen y de los planos de la realidad, lo que equivale a llevar la poesía a un último plano de pureza y sencillez. Se trata de una realidad distinta, dar un salto a mundos de emociones vírgenes, teñir los poemas de un sentimiento planetario [...] Evasión de la realidad por el camino del sueño, por el camino del subconsciente, por el camino que dicte un hecho insólito que regale la inspiración [...] El surrealismo emplea el sueño, el realísimo mundo de los sueños, en donde se dan normas poéticas de verdadera autenticidad, pero esta evasión por medio del sueño o del subconsciente es, aunque muy pura, poco diáfana.

Los españoles queremos perfiles y misterio visible, forma y sensualidades. En el norte puede prender el surrealismo¬ —ejemplo vivo, la actualidad artística alemana—, pero España nos defiende con su historia del licor fuerte del sueño.

Este es mi punto de vista actual sobre la poesía que cultivo. Actual, porque es de hoy. No sé mañana lo que pensaré. Como poeta auténtico que soy y seré hasta mi muerte, no cesaré de darme golpes con las disciplinas en espera del chorro de sangre verde o amarilla que necesariamente y por fe habrá mi cuerpo de manar algún día. Todo menos quedarme quieto en la ventana mirando el mismo paisaje. La luz del poeta es la contradicción. Desde luego, no he pretendido convencer a nadie. Sería indigno de la poesía si adoptara esta posición. La poesía no quiere adeptos, sino amantes. Pone ramas de zarzamora y erizos de vidrio para que se hieran por su amor las manos que la buscan.

TEXTUAL NOTE

7. A manuscript page from Lorca's "Architecture of Deep Song," the revised version of a lecture on deep song he had given for the first time in Granada in 1922 (DS 23-41) and read in New York, Spain, Argentina and Uruguay between 1930 and 1934. By 1930, Lorca could see that cante jondo was not the anonymous, collective creation of the Andalusian people—the vision which prevails in the 1922 lecture—but the individual creation of its performers, and that the best of these had duende. Around the same time (1932-1934) he also speaks of the duende's powers of communication in his public readings of *Poet in New York*. Manuscript: Centro Federico García Lorca.

LORCA READ "JUEGO Y TEORÍA DEL DUENDE" FOR THE FIRST TIME IN the salon of a cultural organization, Amigos del Arte, in Buenos Aires, on October 20, 1933. He read it again for a much larger audience at the Teatro Avenida, Buenos Aires, on November 14; in Rosario, Argentina, on December 22, 1933 with the subtitle "El enigma del alma española," and in Montevideo, on February 6, 1934.

"Duende: Play and Theory" formed part of a series of lectures sponsored by Amigos del Arte: a reading of *Poet in New York*; a musical disquisition on the songs of Granada ("How a City Sings From November to November"); and another on deep song, "Architecture of Deep Song." The lecture on duende—and perhaps some or all of the others—were broadcast on a local station, Radio Stentor (Medina 109). If recordings exist, they have not been found.

The Spanish text given here follows the critical edition of José Javier León (Seville: Athenaica, 2018), which is based on study of the autograph manuscript, a typescript hurriedly corrected by Lorca, and a second copy typed out by Juan Guerrero Ruiz for the lecture's first publication, in volume VII of Lorca's *Obras completas*, prepared by Guillermo de Torre (Buenos Aires: Losada, 1942). I have adapted the notes to "Duende: Play and Theory" from those in the edition of León and in his companion volume, *El duende: hallazgo y cliché*.

"Imaginación, inspiración, evasión" was given for the first time in the Ateneo de Granada, October 11, 1928, a few months after the publication of Lorca's *Primer romancero gitano* (Gypsy Ballads), and delivered again to a progressive women's club—the Lyceum Club— in Madrid, on February 16, 1929 and Bilbao in mid-April, 1929, two months before the poet left for his year-long stay in New York and Cuba. Lorca read it at Philosophy Hall, Columbia University on February 10, 1930, under a new title, "Tres modos de poesía" (Three Modes of Poetry), and in Havana (March 9, 1930), Santiago, Cuba (April 1930) and Cienfuegos (June 4, 1930), under a third title, "La mecánica de la poesía" (The Mechanics of Poetry). In this composite version, I have chosen the first of these titles.

No original or copy of any of these versions has ever been found, and the Spanish text has been pieced together from fragments in newspaper articles found by a number of scholars (Marie Laffranque, Mario Hernández, Daniel Eisenberg, myself, and now Andrew A. Anderson). Some of these offer passages which the reporter took down stenographically and which, whether or not they are enclosed in quotation marks, may be presumed to be accurate transcriptions of the now-lost manuscript from which Lorca was reading. In my edition of García Lorca's *Conferencias* (1984) and in subsequent editions of Lorca's *Obras completas* (by Arturo del Hoyo, Miguel García-Posada, and Andrés Soria Olmedo) those versions are given separately, one after another.

The most complete of the newspaper accounts, from the Bilbao daily *El Liberal* (April 16, 1929, pp. 1-2), recently discovered and generously shared by Anderson, has allowed me to flesh out the lecture with previously unavailable material that was probably either taken down in shorthand or transcribed from the lost original. Combining this new text with those published until now, I have prepared not a critical edition, but what I hope is a faithful adaptation. Rather than presenting the newspaper texts one after another, I am *combining* text from different accounts of the lecture, on different dates, between 1928 and 1930. The passages I have given in italics in this composite adaptation—a textual collage— are clearly journalistic paraphrase rather than direct quotations. All of the newspaper accounts skip from one part of the lecture to another, posing an additional challenge for editors and translators: the order of the paragraphs may have been different in Lorca's original.

8. *Park with Enveloping Line,* ca. 1935-1936. Jean Gebser series, CFGL.

ILLUSTRATIONS

Cover. *Vase on a Roof.* New York, ca. 1929-1930. India ink, pencil and colored pencils. On the reverse of a photo of the poet. 228 x 172 mm. From the collection of Ángel del Río, New York, reproduced with the kind permission of Carmen de Pinies-Hassel.

Frontispiece. Federico García Lorca, on the stage of the Teatro Avenida, Buenos Aires, after the Buenos Aires premiere of *Bodas de sangre* (Blood Wedding), October 25, 1933 (days after he had read his lecture "Duende: Play and Theory"). On the back of the photo, the poet has written a message to his cousin Clotilde García Picossi: "Me. But I don't look good because I was extremely nervous after so many kisses and handshakes. When I went back to the hotel I was too tired to fall asleep. Which explains my false smile—what I wanted was for them to leave me alone. But I see that is impossible. I haven't eaten in the hotel a single day; I constantly get invitations, and people take me here and there. I have had to hire a young man as secretary and typist and to defend me against visitors who get as far as my bed. It's something awful. Buenos Aires has three million inhabitants, but so many photos have come out in these huge newspapers that I am now popular and they recognize me in the street. This I don't like. But it's extremely important for me, because I have won a huge audience for my theater" (*EC* 771-772). CFGL.

1. Federico García Lorca speaking in the Teatro Avenida, Buenos Aires, 1933. Centro Federico García Lorca CFGL 1.1.53.

2. First page of the typewritten manuscript, with autograph corrections, of "Juego y teoría del duende." Pro-7(8) CFGL.

3. *Fabulous Beast Approaching a House.* New York, ca. 1929-1930. India ink and crayons on paper, 357 x 296 mm. From the poet's private collection, preserved by Francisco García Lorca and inherited by Gloria García-Lorca de los Ríos, Madrid.

4. *Rose of Death. Calligram.* Blue ink on paper. Drawing printed on end-leaf of a limited edition of Ricardo E. Molinari's poem *Una rosa para Stefan George* [A Rose for Stefan George], printed in Buenos Aires by Francisco A. Colombo in 1934, during Lorca's visit to Argentina. Cat 291, CFGL.

5. Lorca at a dock at Marianao Beach at Havana, Cuba, 1930. Black and white photograph, 7 x 5 cm. Federico García Lorca Papers, Cuban Heritage Collection, University of Miami Library.

6. *Sight and Touch.* India ink and blue and red colored pencil on paper, 252 x 202 mm. Jean Gebser Series, CFGL.

7. Autograph manuscript page, ca. 1932-33, with comments on duende, from the lecture "Arquitectura del cante jondo" (Architecture of Deep Song), Pro-8(5), CFGL

8. *Park with Enveloping Line, ca. 1935-1936.* India ink on rag paper, 226 x 165 mm. Jean Gebser series, Cat 210, CFGL.

9. *Priapic Pierrot, ca. 1932-1936.* India ink and colored pencils on drawing board, 245 x 184 mm. Jean Gebser series, Cat 200, CFGL.

10. Federico on the stage of the Teatro Avenida, Buenos Aires, October 1933. Photograph, 1.1.44 CFGL.

NOTES

Abbreviations

ACJ   García Lorca, *"Arquitectura del cante jondo"* (lecture)

DS   *Deep Song and Other Prose*

OC   *Obras completas,* edited by Miguel García-Posada (1997)

SA   García Lorca and Dalí, *Sebastian's Arrows*

EC   *Epistolario completo*

Finding Duende

1. For facsimiles of the manuscripts, see the appendix to the León edition.

2. *Juego y teoría del duende.* Study and annotated critical edition by José Javier León, prologue by Andrés Soria Olmedo, Seville, Athenaica, 2018; and José Javier León, *El duende, hallazgo y cliché,* Seville, Athenaica, 1918. The translation given here is a revised version of those published in C. Maurer, tr. *Deep Song and Other Prose,* New Directions, 1980; and *In Search of Duende,* New Directions, 1998. The word "juego" (play) in Lorca's title signals that the poet himself would enact the duende. As Dominique Breton (375) observes, in his lectures on poetics, Lorca both "does what he says and says what he does," entertaining his audiences with what Lorca calls elsewhere "the charming play of poetic emotion that is an inseparable part of the life of the cultivated" (DS 59).

3. Arturo Barea, for example, in *Lorca: The Poet and His People* (1949): "Characteristically Lorca took his Spanish term for daemonic inspiration from the Andalusian idiom. While to the rest of Spain the duende is nothing but a hobgoblin, to Andalusia it is an obscure power which can speak through every form of human art, including the art of personality" (132).

4. Two texts from 1932 contain comments about duende which were later incorporated into "Duende: Play and Theory." In a reading of poems from *Poet in New York,* Lorca tells the audience: "Before reading poems aloud to so many people, the first thing one must do is to invoke the duende. This is the only

way all of you will succeed at the hard task of understanding metaphors as soon as they arise, without depending on intelligence or on a critical apparatus, and be able to capture, as fast as it is read, the rhythmic design of the poem" (*Poet in New York* 182). There are also comments about duende in the version of his lecture "Arquitectura del cante jondo" which he read to audiences in Spain (1932), Argentina (1933) and Uruguay (1934). See *ACJ* 189 ff.

5. In "Corazón bleu y Coeur azul," an imaginary dialogue between himself and Dalí, written in 1927 or 1928, the two discuss the *hecho poético*, and the freeing of objects from the bonds of metaphor and analogy. See Anderson, ed., *Poemas en prosa* 91-92 and *SA* 11-13, as well as Dalí's essay "Reality and Surreality" in Raeburn 225-226.

6. In his letters to his friend the Catalan art critic Sebastià Gasch and elsewhere Lorca carefully distances himself from Surrealism, automatic writing, and the art of dream. On sending him two of his prose poems in September 1928, Lorca writes, "I hope you like them. They answer to my new *spiritualistic* manner, pure, raw emotion, free from logical control, but—careful, careful!—with a tremendous *poetic logic*. This is not surrealism—careful!—they are illuminated by the clearest consciousness" (*EC* 588).

7. On the "intermediality" of Lorca's lecture and aesthetics, see Miguel García, *Queering Lorca's Duende* 10 and *passim*.

Duende: Play and Theory

1. In February 1920 (not 1918) Lorca entered the Residencia de Estudiantes, an elite residential college in Madrid where he would coincide with Luis Buñuel, Salvador Dalí, and a wide range of contemporary poets, painters and thinkers.

2. See introduction, p. 12. In the manuscript Lorca eliminates this anecdote with its echoes of *Don Quixote*: "I remember one [lecture] by a famous fellow whose name I wish to recall but cannot give here; a lecture so tremendous that my roommate, the painter Salvador Dalí, and another two of us, jumped into the swimming pool with all our clothes on."

3. In a reading of his *Gypsy Ballads* in 1935, Lorca uses a similar image: a boring lecture can put "pinpricks in eyes where Morpheus hangs his irresistible anemones" (*OC* III: 178). In a lecture on Góngora, he fears the terrible "botfly of boredom" will get into the room and "string heads together on a slender silken thread" (*OC* III: 53).

4. In the autograph manuscript, Lorca replaces "imágenes brillantes" (brilliant images) with "luces de madera."

5. The image of the Iberian Peninsula as a stretched-out bull's hide, a comparison used by the Greek geographer Strabo, is and was familiar to Spaniards, but not to Lorca's Argentine audience in 1933. The Júcar crosses the Spanish Levant and empties into the Mediterranean. The Pisuerga runs through northern Spain and flows into the Duero, and the Sil, into the Miño in Galicia. The Guadalfeo owes its meager existence to rainfall and to snowmelt from the nearby Sierra Nevada.

6. The Río de la Plata, the broad estuary formed by the confluence of the Paraná and Uruguay rivers, natural border between Argentina and Uruguay. The waters from the Uruguay (the eastern bank) are dark in tone, while the more voluminous Paraná (western bank) is lion-colored. In another speech given in Buenos Aires, Lorca, Lorca refers to the Plata's waves, "reddish and rough as a lion's mane." (*OC* III:225).

7. It was Lorca who popularized the expression *tener duende* (to have duende), superimposing the expressions described in the Introduction (p. 14). In the Southern Cone, in 1933, no one spoke either of duende or of *having* duende in the sense Lorca gives the word. Lorca first uses the expression in his lecture on cante jondo, *ACJ*, in 1932: "The difference between the good cantaor [singer of flamenco] and the bad one is that the good one has duende, what they call duende, and the bad one never achieves that. Duende is the momentary inspiration, the blush of what is alive and being created in the moment. The duende is a fertile force somewhat similar to what Goethe called the demoniacal, and it manifests itself chiefly among musicians and poets of the living voice, more than among painters and architects, because it needs a tremulous instant followed by a long silence" (*Arquitectura del cante jondo*, ed. Maurer 165). *ACJ* was read between 1930 and 1934. The revisions, which were probably made in New York, Havana, and Buenos Aires, have not been definitively dated, but the sentence about duende was probably added before the reading in Buenos Aires. In an interview there on the eve of his lecture, Lorca elaborates: "to have duende is the very dearest thing life can offer to intellectuals. Duende is that magnificent mystery that has to be sought out in the distant dwelling of the blood. [...] These things that appear unhinged in modernist [modern?] poets are efforts to search for duende. One must search for duende; without it, there will be good things in life, but nothing as magnificent as having it. This is the secret of art: to have duende. It wasn't me who invented it, of course; I'm just commenting, because…." The philologist Amado Alonso then interrupts: "Yes, my friend, you're commenting on it because this has very seldom been said, and because it is the means necessary to delve into pure poetry, poetry, painting, and all the arts" (Inglada and Fernández 188).

8. *Torre* ("Tower") : nickname of the cantaor (singer of flamenco) Manuel Soto Loreto, *Niño de Jerez* (Jerez de la Frontera, 1878-Seville, 1933), sometimes referred to as Manuel Torres or Manuel Torre (both spellings can be historically justified.) Torres performed at the cante jondo festival organized by Manuel de Falla and Lorca in 1922. In Seville in December 1927 the poet heard him proclaim, "what you must search for, and find, is the black torso of the Pharoah," a phrase that alludes to the supposed Egyptian origin of the gitanos (cf. Rafael Alberti 266). Lorca used the image in the dedication of a sequence of poems in *Poema del cante jondo* (Poem of the Deep Song), 1931: "A Manuel Torres, 'Niño de Jerez', que tiene tronco de Faraón." When Lorca reads *ACJ* in Buenos Aires (Nov. 8, 1933), he calls Torres "el duende de los duendes." Citing Torres' "grand style," he plays a recording for the audience and remarks floridly: "Manuel, here in beautiful Argentina, I'm playing your voice, captured in the dramatic black moon of the gramophone record, and I hope that, from where you are now, surrounded by immense silence, you will hear the tumult of dahlias and kisses that I want to leave at your feet, as king of cante jondo" (*OC* III: 36) Torres had died destitute in Seville only months earlier and the lecture can be read as a tribute.

9. But it wasn't so in 1933. It was precisely this widely read lecture that spread the concept.

10. Diego Fernández Flores (Lebrija, Seville, 1847-first decade of the 20th century), known also as *Lebrijano el Viejo*. Without documentary proof, Lorca credits him with creating the debla (which was considered a primitive form of deep song, performed without instrumental accompaniment). See Blas Vega y Ríos Ruiz.

11. Alexander Brailowsky (Kiev, 1896-New York, 1976): Russian pianist (nationalized French citizen), a specialist in the Romantic repertory who performed in Granada in 1923 and repeatedly in Montevideo and Buenos Aires in the 1920s. Lorca mentions him again in an interview in Barcelona in 1935, explaining the difference in theater adaptations: "A work by Chopin will be different if played by Rubinstein or by Brailowsky" (Inglada and Fernández, 397). Several of Brailowsky's recodings of Bach are extant.

12. Professional name of Magdalena Seda Loreto (Jerez de la Frontera 1877-Seville, 1956), who performed for more than half a century and was one of the most glorious figures in flamenco. In 1933-34 she was part of the ensemble performing *El amor brujo* (The Love Sorcerer) of Manuel de Falla and *Las calles de Cádiz* (The Streets of Cádiz), works directed by Lorca, the dancer La Argentinita and the bullfighter and impresario Ignacio Sánchez Mejías.

13. *La Malena* might well have uttered such a sentence, but Lorca may be us-

ing the bailaora to express his own judgment (his admiration for Bach is well known.) Something similar happened two years later in 1935 when Lorca took a friend to hear flamenco in the caves of the Sacromonte in Granada. When an old cantaora there stubbornly refused to sing, the poet went home, came back with the family gramophone, and played her some records of Bach. Astonished by the unfamiliar composer, she relented and sang (Gibson 369-70). In the Lorca family record collection are recordings of Bach's second Brandenburg Concerto (Leopold Stokowski) and Cantata no. 4 (Orfeó Català).

14. Ian Gibson believes Lorca is referring to the first movement of *Nights in the Gardens of Spain*, "En el Generalife." Falla had first conceived of his *Nights* as a group of nocturnes for solo piano.

15. The mysterious, radical "black sounds" on which Lorca bases his theory of duende appear five times in the text. In part, they allude to the sound of the black keys on the piano, which may be understood (as José Luis García del Busto points out in an email of 6/9/16) "from two points of view related to harmony: chromatics and the intervals between the black keys, which produce unconventional scales and harmonic ranges that often evoke oriental music, distances, the exoticism of *other musics.*" A less likely hypothesis would be that Torres said "duendes"—"All that has black sounds has duendes"—and that Lorca either misheard him or decided not to hear the bothersome final "s." In the historical musical sense, found in the writing of the musicologist Felipe Pedrell and of the journalist Galerín, there is no doubt that *In the Generalife*, the first movement of *Nights in the Gardens of Spain*, has duendes. The discovery in the archive of Juan Lafita of some maxims by the *Niño de Jerez* proves that, although known for a certain lack of refinement, Torres was familiar with musicological concepts like the semitone.

16. This is not Goethe's definition, but that of his friend Johann Peter Eckermann (Winsen, 1792-Weimar, 1854), apropos of the fourth book of Goethe's autobiography. In the February 28, 1831 entry to *Conversations with Goethe* Eckermann writes of "that controversial force which we all perceive but which no philosopher can explain and which the clergy greet with a consoling word. Goethe calls this unnamable universal and vital enigma 'the demonic' [*Das Dämonische*] and we feel that he truly hits the mark when he defines its essence." When Eckermann asks Goethe whether the daemonic is perceptible in events, he answers: "Particularly, and indeed in all that we cannot explain by reason and understanding. It manifests itself in the most varied manner throughout nature—in the invisible as in the visible. Many creatures are of a purely daemonic kind; in many, parts of it are effective." Asked whether Mephistopheles has daemonic traits, Goethe replies: "No. Mephistopheles is much too negative a being. The Daemonic manifests itself in a thoroughly active power. Among artists, it is found more among musicians—less among painters. In Paganini it shows itself in a high degree and it is thus he produces such great effects." Conversation of March 2, 1831. See also the conversation for March 6, 1831.

17. A curious contrast with Galerín: Lorca's duende "is not in the throat," and Galerín's is located precisely there.

18. On July 2, 1885, Friedrich Nietzsche (Röcken, 1844-Weimar, 1900) writes to his friend the musician Peter Gast (pseudonym of Johann Heinrich Köselitz) that "as I stood still on the Rialto bridge, a music […] touched me to tears, an old tune, so incredibly old that there never seemed to have been an adagio before" (Nietzsche, *Correspondencia* 76), It was there that Nietzsche was inspired to write "Gondellied" or "Venice," published in *Ecce Homo*.

19. On November 27, 1881, Nietzsche attended a performance of Bizet's *Carmen* in the Teatro Politeama of Genoa, an opera he would see more than twenty times and mention enthusiastically in his correspondence. Lorca writes that Nietzsche never found the duende because he was looking for it in the wrong place. Ironically, Nietzsche—like Lorca—was affirming the superiority of the Dionysian over the Apollonian.

20. Silverio Franconetti Aguilar (Seville, 1823-1889), a founding figure in the art of flamenco. In his lecture *ACJ*, Lorca calls him the "portentous […] creator of new styles [i.e., new flamenco genres], the last Pope of deep song, who sung like no one else the song of songs [the siguiriya] and whose cry opened trembling cracks in the moribund mercury of the mirrors." (*OC* III: 52). In *Poema del cante jondo* (Poem of the Deep Song), Lorca alludes to his Andalusian father and Italian mother: "Italy's dense honey / and Spain's lemon / went into the voice of that siguiriyero. / His cry was terrible—/ stood your hair on end, / the old folks say—,/ cracked the backing of mirrors, / passed through modulations / without a single break" (tr. David Loughran). Lorca describes the siguiriya in his two lectures on deep song (1922 and 1930) and makes it the subject of a sequence of poems.

21. Not Nuremberg, but Wartburg Castle, in Eisenach.

22. Jacques Collin de Plancy (246), in his *Infernal Dictionary* (1842) tells of a devil transformed into a dog that got into a convent and "lifted the clothing of the nuns to fool them and incline them to evil" and to what they called "the unspeakable sin."

23. Lorca is probably thinking of the fortune-telling monkey of Maese Pedro, whose prophetic gifts Don Quixote suspects are the fruit of a pact with the devil (*Don Quixote*, second part, Chapter XXVI). The episode was made into

a puppet opera (premiered in 1923) by Lorca's friend and mentor Manuel de Falla.

24. A newspaper account by the journalist Luis Echávarri in the Madrid daily *El Sol*, December 10, 1933 quotes Lorca a bit differently: "the demonic little devil of Descartes who sometimes fled from compasses and numbers and went off to see the orange-colored moon fall asleep in the canals."

25. Three archangels. Lorca had devoted a poem to each of them in *The Gypsy Ballads* (1928), associating Gabriel with Seville, Raphael with Córdoba, and Michael with Granada.

26. The episode of the *Acts of the Apostles* (9: 1-8) which relates the conversion of Saul, mentions not an angel but "a light from heaven." In I *Corinthians* 15:3–8 Christ himself appears to him.

27. According to his earliest biographer, Tommaso da Celano, Francis of Assisi (Assisi, 1181/2-1226), known as "Seraphic Father," felt special reverence for the angels. Various apparitions of angels are associated with him. In the most frequently depicted, one of the seraphim, crucified and suspended in the air, transfers to him Christ's stigmata. As a young poet, Lorca identified with Francis' love of insects and animals despised or ignored by man (*OC* I:487-488) and made him a character in one of his narrative poems (*OC* I: 501-17). In a 1933 radio program in Buenos Aires, he imagines himself, "like the good Franciscan I am," broadcasting "to the clouds, the birds and the melancholy boughs of the jacarandá" (*OC* III: 231)

28. Henry Suso (Constance, 1295-Ulm 1366), Dominican friar, lyric poet and mystic, a disciple of Meister Eckhart, recounts various encounters with angels, both in groups and individually, but mentions no angel as having followed him. Perhaps Lorca was remembering a holy card or engraving. Francisco de Zurbarán portrays eighteen-year-old Suso at the moment of scratching into his breast with a stylus the anagram of Christ, IHS. Since 1836, the painting has been in the Museum of Fine Arts, Seville, which Lorca visited in 1927 and 1935.

29. In 1909 Henri Julien Félix Rousseau (Laval, 1844-Paris 1910), also known as Le Douanier, did two portraits of Guillaume Apollinaire with his lover, the painter Marie Laurencin, titled *The Muse Inspiring the Poet* (Pushkin Museum, Moscow and Kunstmuseum, Basel).

30. In the manuscript Lorca crosses out *rayo* (lightning bolt) and substitutes *langosta de arsénico*. The concatenate ideas and images in this sentence—intelligence as enemy of poetry, artists, insects, the arsenic lobster bequeathed to Lorca by the Surrealists—dialogue with the work of old friends who were, by 1933, reaching new artistic heights: the bee-eaten burro in Buñuel's *Tierra*

sin pan (Land Without Bread), the ants which crawl into and out of the pierced hand in *Un chien andalou* (An Andalusian Dog), Dalí's obsessions with crustaceans… They also chime with the anguish and *aristas* (sharp corners) of Lorca's *Poet in New York* and his Surrealist scenario *Viaje a la luna* (Trip to the Moon). All this is offered in opposition to the monocles, the lacquer rose and the salon—bourgeois, late-Romantic enemies of the duende. There is a similar image in "Imagination, Inspiration, Evasion" (p. 56): inspiration can sometimes "place a livid worm in the clear blue eyes of our muse." In some translations of this text—for example, that of Belitt (156)— *langosta* is translated as "locust" (the word in Spanish can mean either locust or lobster). But as Ignacio Gárate Martínez (41) points out, a passage in one of Lorca's letters to Anna Maria Dalí reinforces the association of the lobster with madness. Distinguishing between the madness of Don Quixote and that of Lydia Noguer, an eccentric denizen of Cadaqués, Lorca writes: "Lydia's madness is a moist, soft madness, full of seagulls and lobsters, a plastic madness. Don Quixote travels through the air, and Lydia, along the Mediterranean shore" (*OC* III: 853).

31. Hesiod's *Theogony*—one of Lorca's favorite books—begins with a proem (verses 1-115) dedicated to the muses, with their "soft, pounding feet." See Maurer, *Jardín deshecho: Lorca y el amor* 142.

32. Lorca associates gold leaf with angels (for centuries, their statues were gilded throughout the Hispanic world) and the tunic fold (the Greek chiton, sometimes pleated) with the muse, though angels too have frequently been depicted as wearing tunics.

33. The three ways of St, John of the Cross are the purgative, illuminative and unitive. In *The Interior Castle, or The Mansions* (1577) Saint Teresa describes the soul not as a tower but as a castle formed of diamantine or transparent crystal, to which one accedes by means of active prayer followed by contemplation. In this guide to meditation the tower appears only as an exhortation, in the final paragraphs of the book. The mystical path consists not of building great towers but of love in action.

34. *Isaiah* II, 45: 15, "Verily thou art a God that hidest thyself, O God of Israel, the Savior."

35. In *Ascent of Mount Carmel* John of the Cross (469) remembers Psalm 118:12, "They surrounded me like bees; They were quenched *like a fire of thorns*": and adds, "the desires, [*apetitos*] which are the thorns, increase the fire of anguish and torment." Lorca's "fiery thorns" or "thorns of fire" might also allude to the devotion of the Sacred Heart of Jesus,

popularized by the Jesuits from the seventeenth century on, in which the heart is shown encircled by thorns and giving off flames. During the 19th century all of Spain heard that three thorns had appeared in the incorrupt heart of Saint Teresa preserved in the Carmelite Monastery of Alba de Tormes.

36. Poetry offers "brambles and splinters of glass" so as to wound the hands of those who love her and look for her ("Imagination, Inspiration, Evasion," p. 60).

37. Reference to the fourteen Black Paintings done on the walls of the Quinta del Sordo between 1819 and 1823, today exhibited in the Prado Museum, Madrid. On Lorca and the Black Paintings, see Hirsch 55-57.

38. Mossèn (Father) Jacint Verdaguer i Santaló (Folgueroles, Barcelona, 1845- Barcelona, 1902), priest and poet who wrote in Catalan and was one of the protagonists of the late Romantic movement called the Renaixença, made summer trips through the Pyrenees in 1882 and 1883 and in 1884 resided at the sanctuary of the Mare de Déu del Mont, in the Alto Ampurdán. The result of those excursions was his epic poem *Canigó* (1886). Lorca's reference to his nakedness seems more metaphoric than anecdotal. Later in the lecture he applies the same adjective to the architect of the Escorial, Juan de Herrera, alluding to his severe style.

39. "...to his town of Ocaña, / came death, knocking / at the door," writes Jorge Manrique (1440-1479) in *Verses on the Death of his Father*, a death Manrique himself witnessed in 1476, three years before his own.

40. "What I liked were: absurd paintings, pictures over doorways, stage sets, carnival backdrops [toiles de saltmbanques]" ("Delirium II. Alchemy of the Word," Rimbaud 232.). "And we will exist, and amuse ourselves, dreaming of monstrous loves and fantastic worlds, complaining and quarreling with the appearances of the world, acrobat [saltimbanque], beggar, artist, bandit—priest!" ("Lightning," Rimbaud 241). Lorca may have been remembering, among many modern representations, Picasso's paintings or Baudelaire's prose poems about saltimbanques—traveling acrobats or circus performers.

41. The Comte de Lautréamont, was the pseudonym of the French poet Isidore-Lucien Ducasse (Montevideo, 1846-París, 1870). In a speech about Pablo Neruda in 1934, Lorca recalls the "sobbing of the Uruguayan and never-French Comte de Lautréamont, whose song fills with horror the early-morning hours of the adolescent" (*OC* III: 250). In the *Chants of Maldoror* (published 1868-69), which seduced the Surrealists and Lorca's friend Dalí, the protagonist is a demoniacal figure who renounces the human and the divine. In Canto II Lautréamont (65) writes: "It is midnight, there is no longer a single omnibus to be seen from the Bastille to the Madeleine. I am mistaken: here is one approaching suddenly as if were emerging from below ground. The few belated passers-by eye it attentively, for it seems unlike any other omnibus. Seated on the open upper deck are men with the immobile eyes of dead fish." Madeleine-Bastille line, Line E, went down the Grands Boulevards.

42. The gitana Pastora Pavón Cruz, *La Niña de los Peines* (The Girl of the Combs) (Seville, 1890-1969), one of the undisputed masters of flamenco, a cantaora much admired by Lorca. In his lecture "Architecture of the Deep Song" (1930), he calls her "a master of sobbing, a creature martyred by the moon or furious bacchante. Green gypsy mask to whom the duende gives the trembling cheeks of a girl just kissed. The voice of this exceptional woman smashes the molds of every school of flamenco, and those of all constructed music. When she seems to be out of tune, it is just the opposite—she is incredibly *in* tune because, thanks to a special miracle of style and passion, she can hit thirds of tones and quarter tones impossible to register on the musical stave" (*OC* III: 37).

43. The bullfighter Rafael Gómez Ortega (Madrid, 1882-Seville, 1960) was in Buenos Aires at the same time as Lorca and a month after giving this lecture, the poet presided over a ceremony in his honor at the Teatro Avenida (see "Homenaje taurino en el Avenida," *Crítica*, Nov 24, 1933). A few months earlier than Lorca, Edgar Neville made much the same comparison between representatives of high culture and popular culture: on June 19, 1933 he published in the Madrid daily *La Voz*, a series of aphorisms in the style of Ramón Gómez de la Serna about the dances of La Argentinita and Rafael Ortega: "The dance of Ortega is as important as the work of Velázquez." It seems more than likely that Federico read those aphorisms. Asked what he would like his own theater to be like, Lorca answered "Popular. Always popular, with an aristocracy of blood, spirit and style but steeped in the popular, nourished by the sap of the people" (*OC* III: 424)

44. A dry white wine made with palomino grape and aged under a film of yeast called 'velo de flor' in the bodegas of Sanlúcar de Barrameda, Cádiz, at the mouth of the Guadalquivir. Manzanilla was probably the most common drink in the taverns and cafés where flamenco was sung.

45. Ignacio Espeleta (Cádiz, 1871-1938), a sharp-witted cantaor whom Lorca met through Ignacio Sánchez Mejías, was in charge of the tripe shop in the Cádiz slaughterhouse. He was known for his laziness and Cádiz for its refinement. When the *Conte Grande* docked in Montevideo, the poet remarked that "Cádiz is the nerve center of Andalucía… There everything hurts… It's a place of refinement and culture, but not the culture of books or machines; a place with culture in the blood" (Inglada and Fernández 182).

46. Several branches of the Rothschild family were elevated to nobility in the 19th century, some by Emperor Francis I of Austria and others by Queen Victoria. The gitana Soledad Vargas, or *Soleá la de Juanelo*, was a pretty singer who performed professionally in cafés (late 19th - early 20th century) and excelled at bulerías and soleares. Lorca probably heard of Elvira *la Caliente* from his friend the bailaor Rafael Ortega. An interview conducted in Lorca's hotel room in Buenos Aires while Lorca's lecture was being copied by his newly-hired typist, Arturo Bazán, provides a curious textual detail. Bazán asks Lorca about a word he cannot read in the poet's difficult handwriting: "Elvira...Elvira...what?" Lorca answers: "Elvira la Caliente [Hot Elvira], the sacred aristocratic name of a Sevillian streetwalker" (Inglada and Fernández 190). Although the autograph manuscript reads "Elvira," the typescript—and subsequent editions—read "Eloisa." For a discussion, see León 2018, pp. 93-97.

47. Previous editors mistakenly read "Floridas" here. The *Guarriros* are Francisco Monge Fernández, *el Guarriro*, and his wife Rita Ortega Feria, *la Rubia*: stylish gypsies with a legendary and tragic aura, uncle and aunt of Rafael Ortega. Francisco was an incomparably extravagant dandy from Málaga, a rich butcher, flamenco impresario and "hermano mayor" (president) of a gitano Holy Week brotherhood; Lorca writes that "he buttoned his shirt with diamonds when receiving the visit of his compadre the great Lagartijo" (*OC* III: 259). Rita was directly related to the famous bullfighters the Gallos, and the descendent of the cantaor Enrique *el Gordo Viejo*. She died young, when she was about to give birth—so the legend goes—bleeding to death on stage in a dance contest with la Mejorana. Lorca mentions her death in a speech introducing Rafael Ortega and Pilar López at the Residencia de Estudiantes in March 1935 (*OC* III: 258-59.)

48. Mythical king of Tartessos, the tricephalic giant who inhabited the island of Erytheia (identified by some with Cádiz or one of its nearby isles), slain by Heracles, whose Tenth Labor was to obtain Geryon's cattle.

49. Lorca's "Pablo Murube" must be Felipe Murube Monge (b. Los Palacios, Seville, 1841), one of the most important flamenco aficionados of his time, backer of the cantaor Antonio Chacón. Lorca knew the Sevillian family well, and stayed at their house, so the mistake is odd.

50. Lorca must have heard the exclamation "Viva París!" from the bailaor Rafael Ortega, who fascinated him. It was also Ortega, whom he called "the quintessential gitano of royal blood" (*OC* III: 258), who told him about the romantic and tragic history of his uncle and aunt, the *Guarriros*.

51. Various people testify to the fact that Pastora Pavón did not drink. Lorca not only says that she gulped down a big glass of cazalla (anise with up to 40% alcohol content), but that she warmed up with manzanilla (see note 44). No wonder she was annoyed when told of this story.

52. The *lucumí* rite refers to *santería*, also known as the Rule Ocha Ifá, the syncretic Caribbean religion that brings together Yoruba and Catholic beliefs. In it, the Yoruba deity Shango is identified with the Catholic Saint Barbara. The paroxistic rending of clothing appears not only in these rites but also in various ancient and modern cultures, from the Ugaritic *Epic of Aqhat* to the narrations of the Old Testament to the Arabic culture of tarab. It also appears among Russian Roma, the wedding ceremony of Spanish gitanos, and in the context of flamenco and bullfighting. The Mexican writer Salvador Novo (307) heard Lorca describe a santería rite he had witnessed in Cuba in 1930: "an authentic ñáñiga ceremony which he paraded before my eyes, leaving till the end of his well-constructed story the suprise that it was a girl from Galicia [...] who did the ritual dance with the same sacred grace that in Spain makes him begin to break bottles and glass and mirrors as a fatal contagion of cante jondo."

53. The image of the voice as jet of blood derives from the fossilized metaphor "un chorro de voz," literally a spurt or jet or outpouring of voice, and in this context, it can be associated with the "decapitated cry of Silverio's siguiriya" and the singing of flamenco in slaughterhouses. Several of Lorca's drawings show a figure vomiting blood.

54. Several Christ figures carved by Juan de Juni show the feet crossed in an unclassical manner, and fastened to the cross with a single spike, with the toes splayed outward.

55. Lorca must have been familiar with the etymology of *entusiasmo* (enthusiasm, from ἐνθουσιασμός, «rapture, ecstasy», and ἐνθουσία, divine inspiration, possession by a God.) In a letter of 1924 he defines enthusiasm as "the wing of the Holy Spirit." (*OC* III: 807). Cf. Óscar Enrique Muñoz (21 ff).

56. In 1925 the *Diccionario de la Real Academia* had derived the word *olé* from *wallāh*, an etymology endorsed by Lorca's friend the Arabist Emilio García Gómez: "The olés we hear in cante jondo come from the *wállâh*, 'by God!', with which the Arabs greet the reciting of poetry" ("Tárab," *ABC* (Madrid), February 1, 1946, p. 3). In his *Breve diccionario etimológico de la lengua castellana* (1973), the philologist Joan Corominas rejected that origin.

57. The generalization is untrue, though the cry—"¡Viva Dios!"—might have been heard in sudden bursts of enthusiasm among members of the Spanish gitano community.

58. In October 1926, in the Athenaeum of Granada, Lorca read a lecture titled "Paradise Closed to Many, Gardens Open to Few," about the homonymous work by the Baroque poet Pedro Soto de Rojas (Granada, 1584-1658). In it he explains how the title of the poem reflects the character of Granada and glosses the seven "mansions" or "gardens" into which the poem is divided (OC III:78-87).

59. Lorca writes mistakenly "Juan Calímaco" but means John Climacus, the 6th/7th-century ascete, author of *Klimax Theias Anodou* (The Ladder of Divine Ascent, translated into Latin as *Scala Paradisi*), a work divided into thirty steps, the seventh of which dealt specifically with "weeping as a cause of true happiness" and as precursor of "the most holy quietude and tranquility found in God." Francisco García Lorca remembers an old edition, bound in vellum, of the *Ladder*, translated by Fray Luis de Granada, that was in the family library. Young Federico copied various passages of this work from steps 4, 9, 10 and 11. His last note is this one: "Perpetual companion of weeping (is silence)." (OC IV: 868).

60. This contest might have been wholly or partially invented by Lorca based perhaps on the dance of *La Malena*, *La Macarrona* and *La Fernanda* with the Spanish Dance Company of Argentinita. All three were from Jerez, septuagenarians, and shared the dance floor with young male and female flamenco dancers.

61. Eleonora Duse (Vegevano, 1858-Pittsburgh, 1924) was one of the most famous actresses of her time. In *The Razor's Edge* (1944) Somerset Maugham has one of his characters say of another who has "a tension, a secret, an aspiration, a knowledge—that sets him apart": "Sometimes he reminds me of a great actor playing perfectly a part in a trumpery play. Like Eleanora Duse in *La Locandiera*." The Catalan actress Margarita Xirgu, leading lady in some of Lorca's plays, knew her personally.

62. Lorca writes Sarasate in the manuscript and later replaces it with Paganini. It is striking that his first intention was to place Pablo de Sarasate (Pamplona, 1844-Biarritz, Francia, 1908)—less fiery as a violinist than the Italian and perhaps more subtle—on the altar of the *enduendados* (those possessed by duende). The celebrated performer and composer Niccolò Paganini (Genova, 1782-Niza, 1840) descended not infrequently to vulgarity, according to those who, without denying his virtuosity, called him exhibitionistic, greedy, and lacking in taste in certain of his own compositions. Goethe met him in 1829 in Weimar during a tour through Germany, but it is not clear that Goethe ever wrote the words Lorca attributes to him.

63. Spanish title of the Neapolitan couplet "Maria, Marì" by Eduardo Di Capua and Vincenzo Russo. The version that Lorca says he heard might have been performed as a flamenco *cuplé por bulerías*, a style able to be alternately sung and danced, which arose precisely around this time. The first one was recorded in 1929 by Manuel Vallejo (Seville, 1891-1960). For the lyrics see León 2018, Appendix 2. The image of the gewgaw converted, thanks to the duende's art, into the phallic and surrealistic "hard serpent of chased gold," suggests a sort of alchemy.

64. Lorca makes a similar observation in his lecture on lullabies: "Spain is the country of profiles. There are no smudgy borders one can cross to flee to the other world. Everything is delineated and bounded very exactly. A dead man is deader in Spain than in any other part of the world. Whoever wants to leap into dream wounds his feet on the blade of a barber's razor." (*DS* 9-10).

65. "The Dream of the Skulls," an expurgated version, published in 1631, of "The Dream of the Final Judgment" (1605), is the first, the briefest, and the most irreverent and obscene of the *Dreams* of Spain's great Baroque poet Francisco de Quevedo. The oil painting to which Lorca is alluding is *Finis Gloriae Mundi* by Juan de Valdés Leal (Seville, 1622-1690), a highly allegorical *vanitas* painted between 1671 and 1782 whose central motifs are the decomposing bodies of a bishop and a knight from the Order of Calatrava. Lorca had alluded to the painting in an early essay on the decoration of sepulchres: "When one looks at a sepulchre, one senses the cadaver inside it, without gums, full of vermin [...] or smiling satanically like Valdés Leal's bishop" (*OC* IV: 107).

66. From the folk "Ballad of the Evil Mother in Law." Don Boyso arrives home while his wife Marbella is giving birth and, angered by suspicions of adultery that his mother has instilled in him, searches her out and orders her to mount his horse. The ballad ends in tragedy: Marbella dies near the hermitage where she had asked for confession, the newborn baby denounces his grandmother before passing away, and don Boyso goes off to search for his mother, orders her placed into a "barrel with spikes" and, pushing it down a hill, puts her to death (Menéndez Pidal 160).

67. A stanza from "Los mozos de Monleón" (The Boys of Monleón) a folk ballad transcribed by Dámaso Ledesma in his *Folk-Lore o Cancionero salmantino* (Salamanca Songbook), a 1907 compilation Lorca knew almost by heart. Playing his own arrangement at the piano, Lorca recorded it in 1931 with the singer Encarnación López Júlvez, *La Argentinita*.

68. A speech Lorca gave before one of the performances of his theater troupe, La Barraca (*OC* III: 219), suggests that the balustrade (barandilla) mentioned here evokes the fresco by Goya in the Chapel of San Antonio de la Florida, Madrid. The saltpeter flowers are a symbol of decay: what Lorca calls (in a

letter of 1926) "the light, the weightless blossoms of saltpeter which float over the old walls of a house neglected by its owner" (OC III:907)

69. Traditionally attributed to Jeremiah, "the weeping prophet," the *Lamentations* are a biblical book of prophecies and elegies for the fall of Jerusalem.

70. In a city like Granada the cypress tree is associated with death and with cemeteries, but also with the convents and enclosed gardens on the hillsides over its rivers, as well as with the Generalife and the Alhambra. Tradition holds that St. John of the Cross meditated and wrote several of his great poems under a rare and majestic variety of the cypress called "Saint John Cypress" (*Cupressus lusitanica* or *Lindleyi*), the White Cedar or Teotlate, brought from México by evangelizing Carmelite monks and planted in the Carmen de los Mártires, Granada, at the beginning of the 16th century by the mystic poet or by one of his brothers. On St. John, cf. OC III:271.

71. In the autograph manuscript Lorca writes: "The ravine evokes the person who has leaped to his death, and the dry tree evokes the man who has been hanged. The bell evokes the coffin, and fresh earth, the body frozen stiff in the darkness."

72. Lorca is referring to the ending of *La Celestina* (1499) by Fernando de Rojas: the agonizing lament of Pleberio and his wife over the death of their daughter Melibea.

73. The poet and dramatist José de Valdivielso (Toledo, 1560?-Madrid 1638) author of allegorical plays (*autos sacramentales*) like *Farsa sacramental de la locura* (Sacramental Farce on Madness) or *El hijo pródigo* (The Prodigal Son), both of which contain examples of the dances mentioned by Lorca. Gárate Martínez (49) singles out *El hospital de los locos* (The Hospital of the Mad), where Lucifer is among those dancing.

74. From a novelesque ballad known by different titles, e.g., "La esposa difunta" (The Dead Wife) and "Aparición de la enamorada muerta" (Apparition of the Beloved). Versions have been collected from different regions of Spain, Argentina, Mexico, California and New Mexico. Lorca quotes from the version titled "Los quintados" ("The Recruits") in Ledesma's *Cancionero salmantino*, but replaces the recurrent expression "my dear Elvira" with "my pretty friend," giving the verses the feel of folk lyric. The ballad tells the story of a recruit whose captain allows him to turn back from battle in order to see his spouse. On the way, a "little traveler" gives him the bad news that his wife has died. As he goes down his path, the dead woman appears to him: "A little farther ahead / he saw a shadow appear. / If you are my dear Elvira, / why don't you look at me, say..."

75. Number 237 in the *Cancionero musical de palacio,* the Renaissance song-book that was an inspiration to Lorca and other poets of his generation. As he did often, Lorca has retouched the anonymous text.

76. It is difficult to say for sure, but Lorca might be thinking of Zurbarán's portraits of saints (Serapio, Bonaventure, Casilda, Isabel of Portugal…) who are illuminated by a high overhead light with white reflections. The same moonlike character is found in some of Zurbarán's crucifixions, several of which are in national museums like the Fine Arts Museum, Seville, and the Prado, Madrid.

77. The life and work of Father José Martínez de Espinosa, better known as fray José de Sigüenza (Sigüenza, 1544-El Escorial, 1606), are tied to the construction of the Escorial. Lorca could be referring to the *History of the Order of Saint Jerome* (1595-1605), a narration which Unamuno considered a "marvel of language and, in certain passages, of poetry" and, like the Escorial itself, "a model of simplicity, of sobriety, of majesty, and of cleanliness." Chapters 20-22 of Part I relate the death and burial of Philip II.

78. The work of Juan de Herrera (Roiz, Cantabria, 1530-Madrid, 1597) in the Basilica of San Lorenzo de El Escorial, with frescoes by Luca Cambiaso representing "The Coronation of the Virgin." The high-altar piece was designed by Herrera. The altar is flanked by the famous cenotaphs of Charles V and Philip II by Leone and Pompeo Leoni.

79. Under the Colegiata de Nuestra Señora de la Asunción in Osuna (Seville), are a pantheon and crypt which have served as the mausoleum of the dukes since the 16th century.

80. The merchant Álvaro Alfonso de Benavente ordered the chapel constructed in 1543 in the church of Santa María de Mediavilla, in Medina de Rioseco, Valladolid. The artwork by Juan and Jerónimo Corral portrays three episodes from Genesis: the creation of Eve, original sin, and expulsion from paradise. In the last one Death is shown as a skeleton who plays a guitar and dances mockingly before Adam and Eve. The image is not as Spanish as Lorca supposes; it is a topos found throughout Europe and all three images have precedents in Hans Holbein the Younger's *Totentanz* (dance of death) drawings (1523), which served as the basis for a series of popular engravings.

81. *A San Andrés de Teixido vai de morto o que no foi de vivo* (whoever has not gone to San Andrés de Teixido while alive goes when dead), says a Galician proverb attesting to the belief that the souls who do not attend the procession to the village church in Teixido (Cedeira, A Coruña) will be reincarnated as animals who inhabit those landscapes: lizards, butterflies, ants, snakes or toads, which the pilgrims take pains not to harm.

82. A song for "departed souls" which Eduardo Martínez Torner transcribed in Llamo, municipality of Riosa, Asturias. The words say, "The souls of Purgatory / are at your door, / If you give us alms / you will be certain of glory. // Ay, ay, ay, I'm burning, / ay, ay, ay! I'm being burnt. / Take pity on our souls , / who are suffering torment." Groups of postulant women sing from door to door on All Hallows' Eve, and spend what they collect on Masses for the souls in Purgatory. Torner writes that they are "covered with black veils from head to toe; the choir is led by two women who carry a burning lamp and a little bell, respectively, with which they punctuate the end of each line of the stanza. The sadness of the melodic phrase in the silence of the night, and all that comes together in this act, make people's souls shrink in fear" (Martínez Torner, song number 173).

83. A medieval liturgical chant and drama prohibited by the Council of Trent in the 16th century whose syncretic text, combining Christian and pagan traditions, features the classical myth of the Erythraean Sybil, who predicts the end of the world and Last Judgment. It was sung in the cathedrals of Toledo, Burgos, Cuenca, and León and is still heard in the midnight Mass on Christmas Eve in the cathedrals of Palma de Mallorca and Alghero (Sardinia) and in the Monastery of Lluc (Mallorca). There are versions in Latin, Catalan and Castilian. Maria Isabel Mininni (106) adds that in 2010, the rite was declared a Masterpiece of the Oral and Intangible Heritage of Humanity by UNESCO.

84. "In *recort* [or *record*] *de la mort i passió de Nostre Senyor Jesucrist*" (In memory of the death and passion of our Lord Jesus Christ): a phrase chanted in Catalan during the procession on Palm Sunday in Tortosa, to the accompaniment of drum and out of tune trumpet. Felipe Pedrell, who participated as a boy in the procession, describes it vividly in his *Cancionero musical popular español* (Casells, Valls, 1918, I, 101-103), one of Lorca's favorite compilations of popular song.

85. Interviewed by the cartoonist Luis Bagaría in 1936, Lorca declares that bullfighting "is probably the greatest treasure of life and poetry that exists in Spain, incredibly neglected by writers and artists mostly because of the false education we received when young and that men of my generation have been the first to reject. I believe that bullfighting is the most cultivated spectacle in all the world: it is pure drama, in which the Spaniard sheds his best tears and his best bile. It is the only place where one can go with the certainty of seeing death surrounded by the most dazzling beauty. What would become of Spanish spring, of our blood and our language if the dramatic fanfare of the bullfight were to fall silent? By temperament and poetic taste, I am a profound admirer of Belmonte" (*OC* III: 639). See also "Poem of the Bull" (*In Search of Duende* 82-85).

86. Cf. Lucretius' *De Rerum Natura*, IV, 710-15. "Why, even the cock, clapping out the night with his wings, who is accustomed to summon the dawn with clear voice, is one before whom ravening lions dare not stand fast or stare: so surely do they think at once of flight, no doubt because there are certain seeds in the cock's body, which, when they are sped into the eyes of a lion, dig holes in the pupils and cause stinging pain, so that they cannot endure against it for all their courage" (Tr. W.H.D. Rouse). Lorca quotes lines 711-13 (about the gallo, or rooster, putting the lion to flight) as an aggressive epigram—directed against the Granadan bourgeoisie—in the first issue of *gallo*, the literary magazine he founded in Granada.

87. The medieval poet Alonso Álvarez de Villasandino is represented in the *Cancionero de Baena* (Baena Songbook) by funeral elegies dedicated to Enrique III and Juan I. The 16th-century poet Fernando de Herrera composed more than 40 elegies. Juan Ramón Jiménez published early books of poetry entitled *Pure elegies* (1908), *Intermediate Elegies* (1909) and *Lamentable Elegies* (1910). The closest thing to an elegy written by Gustavo Adolfo Bécquer would be his ode to the death of Alberto Lista, where he marshals the muses and Apollo to weep for the deceased. In his poem "To Quintana," an archangel asks to crown his brow "with eternal laurel" and the final verses are spoken by an angel. Half a dozen of his *Rimas* have a lugubrious tone. John Keats, who wrote odes, sonnets and epistles, but not a single poem titled "elegy," is associated with that genre through Percy Bysshe Shelley's, "Adonais: An Elegy on the Death of John Keats" and the many poems which commemorated his early death. Lorca himself an elegiac poet, identifies elegy with the true voice of Granada.

88. According to tradition, St. Teresa of Ávila exclaimed, on looking at the portrait Juan de la Miseria had painted of her, "May God pardon you, fray Juan, not only for painting me but for painting me ugly and bleary-eyed." As for bullfighting, Lorca is probably referring to an anecdote he heard from his friend Sánchez Mejías when the latter gave a lecture on bullfighting in New York (Lorca introduced him). The Marquis of San Juan de Piedras Albas tells the story in his *Fiestas de toros. Bosquejo histórico* (Historical Sketch of the Bullfight, 1927), which is dedicated to Sánchez Mejías. For obvious reasons, Teresa would have found it impossible to slap the Papal Nuncio. The adjective "flamenca" is used here in all of its popular senses: pretty, "cool," brave, daring. On Teresa and García Lorca, see J. J. León 2019.

89. Lorca refers to the transverberation St. Teresa tells about in her autobiography: "I saw an angel beside me toward the left side, in bodily form, something I very seldom see. Although angels are often represented to me, it is without seeing them, except in the sort of vision I have already referred to. But in this one it pleased the Lord that I should see him thus: he was not large, but small, very beautiful, his face so blazing with light that he seemed to be one of the very highest angels, who appear all on fire. [...] I saw in his hands a long dart of gold, and at the end of the iron there seemed to me to be a little fire. This I thought he thrust through my heart several times, and that it reached my very entrails" (Walsh 135-136). Lorca's lifelong devotion to the saint is evident in his earliest plays, poems, and prose and in his intention, in 1936, to "give the Spanish theater a mystical, human Santa Teresa," a figure he found "irresistibly attractive" (*Ecos Mundiales*, Mexico, May 1937, p 103.) See J. J. León 2019.

90. Lorca alludes both to Philip's proselytizing Catholicism, which implied a fierce struggle against heresy and the cultivation of theological study, and to his scientific education and interest in astronomy, the impulse behind his research, acquisition of books (he put together the greatest private library in the West), and collection of armillary spheres, astrolabes, compasses, maps, quadrants and sextants, celestial and terrestrial globes and other instruments.

91. Lorca had already stated that the duende "had leapt from the Greek mysteries to the dancers of Cádiz," and he returns here to anachronistic notions shared by a phalanx of modern writers on flamenco. Cf. his eulogy of Antonia Mercé, in *In Search of Duende*.

92. The idea appears for the first time in Lorca's lecture "Architecture of the Deep Song" (1930). The cantaor, he writes, "has a profoundly religious sense of his song. He sings at the most dramatic moments and never for entertainment, as in the great faenas of the bullfight, rather to take flight, to evade, to suffer, to bathe the everyday in a supremely aesthetic atmosphere" (*OC* III:51). Such statements—that one never sings to amuse oneself or that in Spanish dance no one is entertained—are, to say the least, open to debate.

93. There is a similar image in "Architecture of the Deep Song", the lecture in which he first mentions the duende.

94. See Baudelaire, "La chevelure" ("Head of Hair"), verses 13 ff. In a sentence crossed out of the autograph manuscript, Lorca says that the duende "rocks back and forth with the accent of Baudelaire."

95. Lorca's statement would give primacy to the arms, "rounding," symmetries, opposition and rotation of wrists, hands and fingers in the dance designated "from the waist up," historically identified with feminine dance, as distinguished from dance where the expressive movements are concentrated in the play of the hips, legs and feet and whose rhythm (velocity, strength, rhythm) is marked by the percussive *zapateo*. Such binary contrasts (man vs. woman, gitano vs. non-gitano, from the waist up vs. from the waist down) are common in traditional flamenco, but are questioned in the newer languages of dance.

96. Referring to fray Luis de León and the theologians from the University of Salamanca who defended bullfighting, Sánchez Mejías (123) affirms that "it is the angels who lay down the classical norms of bullfighting. And the devil, the norms of the bull's attack. When a bull charges with bad intentions one says that he is the very skin of the devil." Belitt (179) offers help with the bullfighting terms: "*Muleta*: Cloth of scarlet serge or flannel, folded and doubled over tapered wooden stick, used by matadors for defense, the positional manipulation of the bull, 'passes' to demonstrate the dexterity and daring of the fighter, and as an aid in the final kill. *Banderilla*: A small dart with a bannerol for baiting bulls, thrust in a series of three pairs into the withers of the bull in the second phase of the bullfight. *Faena de capa*: 'cape-task'; the sum of work done by matador in third phase of the bullfight."

97. These and other mathematical references to bullfighting (the duende's fight with geometry, etc.) are influenced by Sánchez Mejías's lecture "El pase de la muerte" (referring to a dangerous pass with the cape). See J. J. León 2018, 184-85 and 199-200 and Lorca's *Sun and Shadow*.

98. The manuscript contains an interesting correction. Lorca's first intention was to distribute his duendes among three popular toreros: Lagartijo (Roman), Joselito (Jewish) Belmonte (gitano). On perceiving that Juan Belmonte (Seville, 1892-Utrera, Seville, 1962) was not a gitano or did not answer to that prototype, he added another bullfighter, Joaquín Rodríguez Ortega, *Cagancho* (Seville, 1903-Mexico, 1941), who was, in fact, gitano, and he called Belmonte "Baroque": an aesthetic distinction, rather than the original ethnic one. On the "statuary aesthetic" of Lagartijo and the emotion provoked by Belmonte, see "Sol y sombra" (Sun and Shadow), *OC* III: 295.

99. The polychromed granite figures in the Pórtico de la Gloria of the cathedral of Santiago de Compostela, a work of the last third of the twelfth century attributable to Maestro Mateo.

100. In various sonnets Lope de Vega (Madrid, 1562-1635), one of Lorca's favorite poets and playwrights, evokes the individual or collective presence of nymphs, naiads, dryads, etc. Lorca appears to suggest that in the religious poems of Lope, the duende purges the erotic inclinations of his profane poetry.

101. The "tower of Sahagún" is that of the church of San Tirso in Sahagún (León). Mudéjar, an exclusively Hispanic style which incorporated into Christian buildings Islamic decorative and architectural ornament and techniques, using brick—associated with andalusí masonry—as construction material. Mudéjar architecture is represented here in the triangle Sahagún (León), Teruel and Calatayud (Zaragoza) but is found throughout Spain.

102. *The Devil-Possessed Constable*, the second of Quevedo's *Dreams*, was probably written in 1607 and was published in 1627. Its narrator is a devil. Goya neither sketched nor painted a *quimera* in the strict sense of the word, an "imaginary monster which vomited flames and had the head of the lion, the belly of a goat and the tail of a dragon" (*Diccionario de la lengua española*) but, figuratively speaking, many of his *Caprichos* could be considered to show chimerae, as could some of his smaller paintings.

103. See note 38.

104. The Castilian sculptor Alonso Berruguete (1488-1561). Lorca particularly admired his *San Sebastián* (*EC* 374 and *SA* between pp. 96 and 97). Lorca's lecture, and the image of the flames, served as inspiration for the film *Fuego en Castilla* (Fire in Castile, 1956-1959) by José Val del Omar (Granada, 1904-Madrid, 1982).

105. Lorca is quoting from stanza 13 of the *Cántico espiritual*. Roy Campbell offers a rhymed version: "The wounded stag above / The slope is now in sight, / Fanned by the wind and freshness of your flight." In an interview with Alberto F. Rivas conducted in his hotel room in Buenos Aires in October 1933, Lorca declared: "Once they asked me what poetry was and I answered, 'Poetry? Well, it's the coming together of two words which no one suspected could be joined, and which produce something like a mystery, and are more suggestive the more they are pronounced; for example, remembering a certain friend, poetry is 'wounded stag.'" (Inglada and Fernández 187). In "Imagination, Inspiration, Evasion" San Juan is the prototype of the inspired poet, best able to evade imaginative convention.

106. The poet Jorge Manrique (c. 1440-1479) fought for Isabel I against Enrique IV and was fatally wounded in a skirmish near the Castle of Garcí-Muñoz, not in Belmonte. Lorca remembers Manrique's verses on the death of his father when writing his own great elegy, *Llanto por Ignacio Sánchez Mejías* (Lament for the Death of a Bullfighter.)

107. Lorca's taxonomy and cartography of the duende of polychromed wood carving, which comes to an end in this paragraph, includes: 1) the Castilian school, centered on Valladolid: Gregorio Hernández (Sarria, Lugo, 1576-Valladolid, 1636), muse; Alonso Berruguete (Paredes de Navia, Palencia, c. 1490-Toledo, 1561) and Juan de Juni (Joigny, Francia, 1506-Valladolid, 1577), duende; 2) the school of Granada: José de Mora (Baza, Granada, 1642-Granada, 1724), angel; Pedro de Mena (Granada, 1628-Seville, 1659), duende; and 3) the school of Seville: Juan Martínez Montañés (Alcalá la Real, Jaén, 1568-Sevilla, 1649), duende.

108. Quevedo and Cervantes, who had already promenaded through this reredos, crown it in its final minute. The first page of the autograph manuscript suggests that Quevedo was going to take pride of place in the lecture: "I'm going to see whether I can show you one of the dark anemones with which Francisco de Quevedo adorned the aching head of Spain." Lorca corrected the sentence in the typescript. Quevedo makes three appearances in this speech, the same conceded to Manuel Torres and to Saint John of the Cross. Only Goya has more mentions (four) than these. As for Cervantes, Lorca declared in an interview in *La Nación* (Buenos Aires, 21-X-1933) that Cervantes "had a gigantic duende but so great was his serenity that it seemed to popular consideration exactly as though he had never had one" (Inglada and Fernández 187-188).

109. The Cave of Montesinos, where Don Quixote did penance, is situated in the Lagoons of Ruidera, in La Mancha, which are the remains of pits from which gypsum was extracted, scorched, and then ground in wind-powered mills. The anemones and phosphorus allude to the infernal *Sueños* (Dreams) of Quevedo. "Plaster flowers" are those affixed as adornments both to the walls and the ceilings of houses, and to the reredos and vaults of Baroque churches.

110. The lecture comes to a sculptural and allegorical resolution in the very Hispanic image of the *retablo* or reredos—the structure situated behind the altar in Roman Catholic Churches, where, by means of painting and/or sculpture, biblical or hagiographical stories are reproduced.

111. Lorca's handwriting here is unclear in the autograph manuscript, but I read *uncen* (to yoke together) rather than the *unen* (unite) of previous editors.

112. Many of the paintings of muses found at Pompei—those of Euterpe, Clio, Terpsichore, etc.—can be said to have "cow's eyes." The painting by Picasso may be one of the portraits of Marie-Thérèse Walter painted between 1928 and 1933.

113. Antonello di Giovanni d'Antonio, called Antonello da Messina (Messina, ca. 1430-1479), a painter of refined technique, master of detail (in hair or objects but also in the landscapes which serve as background to his portraits). The Florentine Fra' Filippo (di Tommaso) Lippi (Florence, 1406-Spoleto, 1469) painted a good number of "annunciations" and the archangel Michael appears in all of them. His panel *The Coronation of the Virgin* (Galleria degli Uffici) and the later fresco with the same theme for the cathedral of Spoleto portray the splendor of a beautiful, well-ordered world with an abundance of angels.

114. Masolino da Panicale (Panicale, 1383-San Giovanni Valdarno, 1440), born Tommaso di Cristoforo Fini, a collaborator of Ghiberti and later of Masaccio and the latter's helper in the extraordinary frescos of the Brancacci Chapel in Florence. In his *Assumption of the Virgin* (1423-8) in the Museo de Campodimonte, Naples, are four angels playing stringed instruments, one of them with a violin.

115. Henri Rousseau, chiefly known as a painter, was a self-taught musician who composed waltzes and gave concerts for his friends in his Parisian home. He retired as a customs inspector at the age of 49 in order to dedicate himself to painting, but his retirement pension was a small one, and he complemented by teaching art or violin and even playing his instrument in the streets.

Imagination, Inspiration Evasion (pp. 51-60)

1. Mario Vargas Llosa (149) once wrote that Lorca "had one obsession. Do not bore the audience. He never did." In 1929, a journalist in *El Pueblo Vasco* took the matter even further: the enthusiastic reaction of Lorca's predominantly female audience proved "that our people are not as positivistic and prosaic as people think" and that Bilbao "is not hermetic [sic] to Poetry or to good poets" (April 16, 1929, 1). According to an account in *Diario de la Marina* (Havana), in his 1930 reading of this lecture (retitled "*Mecánica de la poesía*" (The Mechanics of Poetry), Lorca began by recalling his own parodies of lecturers who had visited the Residencia de Estudiantes, "from the delightful [G.K.] Chesterton with his wire-shavings hair to one-armed [Blaise] Cendrars who sketched the ancient idols, and from Mister [Howard] Carter, dry as the mummy of an Egyptian cat, to the classical Paul Valéry, whose monocle kept turning into a butterfly, to his great displeasure." "This morning," he continued, "with my friends, I'll parody myself and save myself from the literary tone and the delicate, inevitable pedantry of the lecturer." Carter had lectured in November 1924 on the tomb of Tutankhamun; Valéry, in May 1924 on Baudelaire and his descendants; Cendrars, in April 1925 on "Black Literature"; and Chesterton, in April 1926 on the modern novel.

2. Charles-Édouard Jeanneret, Le Corbusier (1887-1965) lectured at the Residencia de Estudiantes on May 9 ("Architecture, Furnishings, and Works of Art") and May 11 ("A House-A Palace"), 1928, arguing for non-decorative functional architecture. While in Madrid, he attended a bullfight, where he might have heard the expression *dar la estocada* (in another newspaper account *dar una estocada*): to plunge the sword cleanly and lethally into the back of the bull's neck. Lorca compared watching the *estocada* to looking at paintings by Miró, "the purest art that has ever been invented": "I experience the same mysterious, terrible emotion I feel at the bullfight at the moment they drive a dagger into the neck of the lovely animal—the moment when we peer over the edge into death, which sinks its steel beak into the tender, intangible trembling of the grey matter" ("Sketch of the New Painting", *SA* 178).

3. Nadine Ly (381) observes that Lorca's statement "turns writing into a blood act" (*un acto de sangre*) and that the meaning of the poem will be the death of the theme. "To write is simply to kill the theme, and to kill it every time it appears before the sword of the poet/matador."

4. In the earliest version of this lecture (Granada, October 1928), Lorca is reported to have said that the "sharpening wheel of all literary history" runs through these three stages or *etapas*: "toda la historia literaria, en su rueda de finar para volver a empezar" (*OC* III: 98).

5. Lorca uses a nearly identical introduction in his essay "On Lullabies" (*DS* 7), given for the first time in 1928, like this one, and repeated in Cuba in spring 1930.

6. A Havana journalist summarizes: "La poesía se recibe; la poesía no se analiza, la poesía se ama." ("Poetry shouldn't be understood, but received; not analyzed, but loved") (*OC* III:10).

7. Lorca develops the metaphor of the hunt for images—and their subsequent "classification" and "selection"—in his lecture on Góngora: "The poet who is about to make a poem (and I know this from experience) has the vague feeling he is going on a nocturnal hunting trip in an incredibly distant forest." Góngora, master of metaphor, and of the hunt for imagery, is Lorca's paragon of the poet of imagination (*DS* 72).

8. A letter to Sebastià Gasch mentions creation not as hunting but as fishing. Speaking of his drawings, Lorca writes: "Some emerge just like that, like the most beautiful metaphors, and others by searching for them in a place where one is certain they are. It is fishing. Sometimes the fish enters the creel on its own, and at other times one looks for the best water and throws out the best hook, so as to make that happen. The hook is called *reality*" (letter of September 2, 1927, *EC* 519).

9. Again, Lorca seems to be thinking of Góngora, who "hates what is deaf," "hates dark forces that have no limits," and "needs the elements to be conscious" (*DS* 80).

10. Lorca's notion of "pure poetry" derives from the *Purisme* expounded by Edouard Jeanneret and Amédée Ozenfant in *After Cubism* (1918) and in the pages of the journal *L'Esprit Nouveau*, read eagerly by Dalí, but would also remind his listeners of the controversial ideas of the Abbé Henri Brémond (expressed in *La poésie pure*, 1926, and other works). In "Sketch of the New Painting" Lorca offers a genealogy: "From Cézanne came the constructive

yearning that would renew painting. Its scaffolding reached acute extremes in Ozenfant and Jeanneret with the style called Purism, and reached scientific extremes in Constructivism, which affirms that 'one cannot determine the boundary between mathematics and art, and between an object of art and a technical invention.' All this brought about a psychological reaction, a spiritualist mode where images are no longer produced by the imagination, rather by the unconscious—by pure, direct inspiration" (*SA* 168).

11. Lorca's friend Guillermo de Torre (131-132), author of an influential history of the European avant-gardes (1925), describes the "Cubist poem" as "pure lyricism [...] with its own origin and climate, ruled by laws born of its own original essence and quality."

12. An idea attributable to the *Purisme* of Jeanneret and Ozenfant (Silver 167). The insistence on the poetic superiority of science over mythology signals Lorca's growing distance from the poetics of Góngora, whom he had praised for his ability to transform traditional myths (*DS* 77). In a lecture on *The Gypsy Ballads* Lorca insists proudly on his own mythopoesis, noting that in his book "myth is mixed with what we might call the 'realistic' element' [...] The book begins with two invented myths, the moon as a deathly ballerina and the wind as a satyr" (*DS* 107).

13. Lorca might be thinking of a geological formation in the midst of a towering pine forest near Cuenca—the Ciudad Encantada—mentioned, years later in one of his *Sonetos del amor oscuro* (Sonnets of Dark Love). Writing to his lover, the poet asks: "Did you like the city the water carved / drop by drop in the midst of the pines?"

14. The reference to sound—singing, the echo—and "cruel swimmers" suggests Lorca is thinking of the Sirens, but associating them with river creatures; or of Hylas, who was captured by nymphs and turned into an echo.

15. The reporter for *El Imparcial* (Madrid) claims to quote Lorca directly: "El eclipse es una fórmula de higiene astronómica que vence el ámbito de las conjeturas" (The elcipse is a formula for astronomical hygiene that surpasses the realm of conjecture.") (Anon, *El Imparcial*).

16. Lorca's first play, *El maleficio de la mariposa* (The Butterfly's Evil Spell), a notable commercial and critical failure, was the fable of a cockroach in love with a wounded butterfly.

17. The poet Robert Bly once remarked that Lorca himself is always saying "what he wants, what he desires, what barren women desire, what water desires, what gypsies desire, what a bull desires just before he dies, what brothers and sisters desire" (Lorca, *Collected Poems* xxxv).

18. Lorca's "Ode to the Most Holy Sacrament of the Altar," published in part in December 1928, two months after he delivered this lecture in Madrid, addresses the three enemies of the soul according to Christian theology: the World, the Flesh, and the Devil (*OC* I: 463-469). In a speech from May 1929, Lorca speaks of his own struggle with his heart, the World and with poetry. "With my heart, to free it from the impossible passion that is destroying it, and *from the deceitful shadow of the World*, which sows it with sterile salt; and with poetry, to construct—though she defends herself like a virgin—a true, wide-awake poem where beauty and horror and the ineffable and the repugnant coexist and collide with one another amid the most radiant joy" (*OC* III: 195-196; italics mine.)

19. Andrew A. Anderson points out that Lorca uses the expression "lógica poética" almost certainly for the first time in a letter to a friend describing someone's prose in August 1927 (email July 2023).

20. *La destronada poesía*. In "Duende: Play and Theory (p. 25)" Lorca warns against intelligence, which can lift the poet to a sharp-edged throne and make the poet impervious to the irrational.

21. In the Madrid version of the lecture, Lorca is reported to have said that the *hecho poético* cannot be controlled, and that one must accept it as one accepts a star shower, and feel happy that poetry can escape, can evade the cold claws of reason. (El hecho poético no se puede controlar con nada. Hay que aceptarlo como se acepta la lluvia de estrellas. Pero alegrémonos–agrega–de que la poesía pueda fugarse, evadirse, de las garras frías del razonamiento.) (*OC* III:104).

22. I have added the final words of this sentence ("age-old irony...") from the Bilbao version of the lecture, where Lorca points out that the poet must struggle with "la ironía vieja y requetevieja, resabiada en los pecados del mundo, que se burla de la inocencia poética, que se presenta desnuda y no quiere justificarse." A Cuban journalist quoted by Dobos (37) writes that Lorca "referred to the irony of certain contemporary lyric poets, who, wishing at times not to reveal certain states of the soul in all their naked purity, disguise them with a touch of irony."

23. Juan Larrea, "Razón", en *Favorables París Poema* I (July 1926): "Y esto que me llega a mí en calidad de inocencia hoy…"

24. The idea of the poetic theorem (the title he gave to at least four of his drawings) came to Lorca, perhaps, from the French critic and cinematographer Jean Epstein, whom Lorca quotes as saying that the metaphor "is a theorem in which one jumps directly from the hypothesis to the conclusion" (*DS* 66).

25. The phrase *hecho poético*, "poetic fact," also connotes "poetic deed," or "event." For the history of this expression, see "Lorca at the Crossroads" by Andrew Anderson 1991 (152-156), who notes that it had been used or quoted, with different shades of meaning, by Epstein and by Le Corbusier (*fait esthétique*), and by Dalí, who speaks of the *hecho poético* (*fet poetic* in Catalan) in several texts and begins one of his essays with an epigraph by Corbusier: "...plus forte est la poésie des faits. Des objets qui signifient quelque chose et qui sont disposés avec tact et talent créant un fait poétique" (stronger is the poetry of facts, of objects which can mean anything and which are arranged skillfully, with talent, creating a poetic fact.) In another lecture, Lorca expresses chagrin over misreadings of his *Gypsy Ballads*, but recognizes that "a poetic fact or event [*hecho poético*], like a criminal one or a juridic one, must exist in the world, must necessarily be bandied about and interpreted" (*DS* 105).

26. An echo of Dalí's letter to Lorca: "Ugly? Beautiful? Words that have lost their meaning. Horror... that's something else" (*SA* 103). Lorca is surely thinking here of his "Ode to the Most Holy Sacrament of the Altar" and of the prose poems he had written in 1927 and 1928.

27. All of these lines are from "Romance sonámbulo" (Sleepwalking Ballad), which Lorca describes as "a pure poetic fact, or event [*hecho poético*] of Andalusian essence," one which "will always have changing lights, even for me, the man who communicated it. If you ask me why I wrote, 'A thousand crystal tambourines / were wounding the dawn,' I will tell you that I saw them in the hands of angels and trees, but I will not be able to say more; certainly, I cannot explain their meaning. And that is the way it should be. By means of poetry a man more rapidly approaches the cutting edge that philosopher and mathematician turn away from in silence" (*DS* 111-112).

28. In the New York version of the lecture, the reporter writes: "[Lorca] analyzes some poems from the *Gypsy Ballads* where there is an infinite number of pure, inexplicable 'poetic facts,' sometimes little noted because [the ballads] are in the line of imaginative poems" ("Analiza algunos poemas del *Romancero gitano* en que hay infinidad de 'hechos poéticos' puros, inexplicables, a veces poco notados por estar en la línea de poemas imaginativos.")

29. Andrés Soria Olmedo (lxx-lxxi) points out that a similar "double equation of pure poetry" is present in a review by Lluís Montanyà of Lorca's *Canciones* (Songs) (1927). According to Montanyà, Lorca strikes a balance between "Intelligence-algebra-geometry = Mallarmé/Valéry/Góngora" on the one hand, and "intuición- sueño-subconsciente = Rimbaud, Lautréamont/Éluard/ St. John of the Cross," on the other.

30. In 1927, in Seville, Lorca and other poets of his generation commemorated with lectures, talks and poetry readings the 300th anniversary of the poet's death. By 1928-30 Góngora no longer seems the greatest of poets. If one can trust a 1933 interview, however, that judgment underwent revision. Asked for his opinion of Paul Valéry, Lorca responds that his poems are "academic, geometrical, impeccable," and quotes a line from his *Cimétière marin.* "Paul Valéry has imagination, an extraordinary imagination, but not inspiration. It is so difficult to bring the two miracles together—the inner and the outer—into a single miracle…The immortal paradigm of that triumph is D. Luis de Góngora" (Inglada and Fernández 128).

31. A few years later (1933) Lorca wrote the opposite: "When the impressionists make landscapes into pap, Cézanne raises definitive walls and paints eternal apples that the cold worm will never penetrate" (*OC* III:243).

32. The poets Juan Larrea (1895-1980) and his friend Gerardo Diego (1896-1987), who maintained an interesting correspondence about poetics, were disciples of the Chilean poet Vicente Huidobro (1893-1948), founder of an avant-garde movement (*Creacionismo*) whose insistence on non-representational art and surprising imagery can be felt in Lorca's writing about the *hecho poético.* See Anderson 1991, 157-158. It was for a celebrated anthology edited by Diego in 1932 that Lorca wrote a statement on his poetics: "In my lectures I've sometimes spoken about Poetry, but what I can't speak about is my own poetry. And not because I'm not aware of what I'm doing. On the contrary: if it's true that I'm a poet by the grace of God—or the devil—, it's also true that I'm a poet by grace of technique and effort and knowing full well what a poem is" (*OC* III:308).

33. The account in *El Imparcial* (Madrid) has Lorca citing Juan Ramón Jiménez as, "without a doubt, the illustrious inspiration for this poetic movement—we will not call it a 'school' so as not to make it something static" (*OC* III: 106).

34. As Anderson (1991) has noticed, Lorca is echoing Dalí's letter to him of October-November 1927: "Until now the metaphor and the image have been anecdotal. So much so that even the purest, most unforgettable of images can be explained like a riddle" (SA 84) In an August 1927 letter (*EC* 513), Lorca writes, "As soon as I pick up my pen to draw, I become unimaginably abstract. I cannot stomach the anecdotal."

9. *Priapic Pierrot*, ca. 1932-1936. India ink and colored pencils on drawing board. One of a series of drawings Lorca made for the German philosopher Jean Gebser, now in the CFGL, Granada: a good example of his art of "evasion." Lorca writes his friend Sebastià Gasch: "I propose themes to myself before I begin to draw, and I get the same result as when I am thinking of nothing. / At these moments I find myself with an almost physical sensibility that carries me off to places where I can hardly remain on foot and am almost flying over the abyss. It's quite difficult to carry on a normal conversation with these people [in Lanjarón] because my eyes and words are someplace else. They are in the huge library that no one has read, in a cool, fresh atmosphere where things dance on one foot" (letter of August 1927, *EC* 516).

A few weeks later, in a letter about dream and the unconscious, he adds: " I have *circled around* dream on some days, but without ever falling entirely into it and always with a safety rope of laughter and sturdy wooden scaffolding. I never venture onto terrains that do not belong to man, because I turn back immediately and almost always tear up the product of my journey. When I do something that is pure abstraction, it always carries a passport of smiles and keeps a rather human balance" (*EC* 518).

BIBLIOGRAPHY

Editions and Translations Consulted

Juego y teoría del duende / Duende: Play and Theory

García Lorca, Federico. "Teoría y juego del duende" [sic], in *Obras completas*, Vol.
    VII. Edited by Guillermo de Torre. Buenos Aires: Losada, 1942: 141-156.
___. "The Duende: Theory and Divertissement," in *Poet in New York*.
    Translated by Ben Belitt. New York: Grove Press, 1955: 154-166.
___. "Théorie et jeu du 'duende,'" in Federico García Lorca, *Oeuvres complètes*,
    Edited and translated by André Belamich. Vol. I. Paris: Gallimard, 1981:
    919-931.
___. *From The Havana Lectures 1928. Theory and Play of the Duende and
    Imagination, Inspiration, Evasion*. Translated by Stella Rodríguez. Preface
    by Randolf Severson. Introduction by Rafael López Pedraza. Dallas, TX:
    Kanathos, 1981: 36-80.
___. "Juego y teoría del duende," in *Conferencias*, vol. II. Edited by Christopher
    Maurer. Madrid: Alianza Editorial, 1984: 85-109.
___. "Jeu et théorie du duende" in Ignacio Gárate-Martínez. *Le duende. Jouer sa
    vie, suivi de Jeu et théorie du duende*. Forward by Xavier Audouard. Paris:
    Encre Marine / Gemme Éditions, 1996, 37-57.
___. "Juego y teoría del duende," in *Obras completas*. Vol. III *Prosa*. Edited
    by Miguel García-Posada. Barcelona: Galaxia Gutenberg / Círculo de
    Lectores, 1997: 150-162.
___. "Play and Theory of the Duende," in *In Search of Duende*. Prose
    selections edited and translated by Christopher Maurer. New York: New
    Directions, 1998.
___. *Gioco e teoria del duende*. Edited, translated and with a commentary by
    Maria Isabella Mininni. Como-Pavia: Ibis, 2016.
___. *Teoría del duende*. [Catalogue of an exhibition at the Centro Federico
    García Lorca, October 30-January 10, 2016, with a facsimile reproduction
    of the original typescript of the lecture]. Consorcio Centro Federico
    García Lorca, 2016.

___. *Juego y teoría del duende.* Study and annotated critical edition by José Javier León. Prologue by Andrés Soria Olmedo. Seville: Athenaica, 2018.

___. *Jeu et théorie du Duende.* Translated by Line Amselem. Paris: Éditions Allia, 2019.

___. "Juego y teoría del duende," in *Obras completas,* vol. I (*Prosa y poesía*). Edited by Andrés Soria Olmedo. Madrid: Biblioteca Castro / Fundación José Antonio Castro, 2019: 190-203.

___. "Juego y teoría del duende," in *Federico García Lorca de viva voz: Conferencias y alocuciones.* Edited by Víctor Fernández y Jesús Ortega. Madrid: Debolsillo, 2021: 229-244.

Imaginación, inspiración, evasión / Imagination, Inspiration, Evasion

García Lorca, Federico. "Imaginación, inspiración, evasión," in Federico García Lorca, *Obras completas.* 2nd edition. Edited by Arturo del Hoyo. Madrid: Aguilar, 1955: 1543-1548.

___. *Oeuvres complètes.* Edited and translated by André Belamich. Vol. I. Paris: Gallimard, 1981: 919-931.

___. *From The Havana Lectures 1928. Theory and Play of the Duende and Imagination, Inspiration, Evasion.* Translated by Stella Rodríguez. Preface by Randolph Severson. Introduction by Rafael López Pedraza. Dallas, TX: Kanathos, 1981: 51-58.

___. *Conferencias,* vol. II. Edited by Christopher Maurer. Madrid: Alianza Editorial, 1984: 11-31.

___. "Imagination, Inspiration, Evasion," in *Sebastian's Arrows. Letters and Mementos of Salvador Dalí and Federico García Lorca.* Edited and translated by Christopher Maurer. Chicago: Swan Isle Press, 2004: 153-162.

___. "Imaginación, inspiración, evasión," in *Obras completas,* vol. I (*Prosa y poesía*). Edited by Andrés Soria Olmedo. Madrid: Biblioteca Castro / Fundación José Antonio Castro, 2019: 190-203.

___. "Imaginación, inspiración, evasión," in *Federico García Lorca de viva voz: Conferencias y alocuciones.* Edited by Víctor Fernández and Jesús Ortega. Madrid: Delbolsillo, 2021: 127-144.

Selected Newspaper Accounts of "Imaginación, inspiración, evasión"

"Vida cultural. El Ateneo de Granada inaugura el curso 1928-29. Conferencia de F.G.L." *El Defensor de Granada,* October 12, 1928.

"Vida cultural. Las conferencias de ayer. 'Inspiracion, emoción. [sic] imaginación.'" *El Imparcial* (Madrid), February 17, 1929.

"Vida cultural. Conferencia de F.G.L. en el Lyceum," *La Época* (Madrid), February 18, 1929.

"Conferencias y reuniones, F.G.L. en el Lyceum." *El Sol* (Madrid), February 19, 1929: 2.

"Mirador Bilbaino. García Lorca en el Ateneo." *El Pueblo Vasco* (Bilbao). April 16, 1929: 1.

"García Lorca, en el Ateneo." *Euzkadi* (Bilbao) April 16, 1929: 3.

"García Lorca en el Ateneo." *El Noticiero Bilbaino*, April 16, 1929: 2.

"García Lorca en el Ateneo." *Gaceta del Norte* (Bilbao), April 16, 1929: 5.

"El poeta Federico Garcia Lorca en el Ateneo." *El Liberal* (Bilbao), April 16, 1929: 1-2.

"F.G.L. en el homenaje que le tributó Columbia University." *La Prensa* (New York), February 12, 1930.

C.M.L. "'La mecánica de la poesía' sirvió de tema al poeta español Sr. F. García Lorca para su conferencia." *Diario de la Marina* (Havana), March 10, 1930: 12.

"El notable poeta lírico español disertó ayer ante los socios de la Institución Hispano-Cubana de Cultura sobre la mecánica de la poesía..." (unidentified clipping, Centro Federico García Lorca.)

Selected Newspaper Accounts of "Duende: Play and Theory"

Rivas, Alfredo F. "Rossini fue cocinero y músico con mucho de eso que llaman 'duende'. García Lorca agrega que os modernistas procuran obtener 'ese no sé qué'" *La Razón* (Buenos Aires), October 21, 1933: 5. Reprinted in Inglada and Fernández, 186-189.

Echavarri, Luis. "La visita de un poeta español y su duende," *El Sol* (Madrid), December 10, 1933: 4.

Robledal, Narciso. "El duende se hizo carne…La extraña confesión del poeta García Lorca," *Aconcagua. El Magazine para Todos* (Buenos Aires) 47 (December 1933): 53-56 and 137. Reprinted in Inglada and Fernández, 186-189.

Other works consulted

Aguilera Sastre. "*Tournée* de García Lorca por los ateneos del norte de España (diciembre de 1930)." *Revista de Literatura* LXXVII: 154 (July-December, 2015): 423-445.

Alberti, Rafael. *La arboleda perdida*, Buenos Aires, Fabril, 1949.

Anderson, Andrew A. "Imagery and How it Works in Lorca's *Poeta en Nueva York*. The Case of '1910 (Intermedio)'." *Forum for Modern Language Studies* 57:1: 1-20.

___. "Introducción," in *Poemas en prosa* de Federico García Lorca. Edited by Andrew A. Anderson. Granada: La Veleta, 2000: 9-53.

___. "Lorca at the Crossroads: 'Imaginación, Inspiración, Evasión' and the 'Novísimas Estéticas'." *Anales de La Literatura Española Contemporánea* 16 (1/2) (1991): 149–73.

Barea, Arturo. *Lorca: The Poet and His People*. New York: Harcourt, Brace, 1949.

Bécavin, Anne-Lise. "Conferencias de Federico García Lorca. Espejo de una época y expresión de una teoría de la creación artística." Thesis, Université Angers, 2014.

Bianchi Ross, Ciro. *García Lorca: Pasaje a la Habana*. Barcelona: Puvill, 1997.

Blas Vega, J. and Ríos Ruiz, M. *Diccionario enciclopédico ilustrado del Flamenco*. Madrid: Cinterco, 1988.

Breton, Dominique. "Jeu, duende, sacrifice : l'autre scène de l'écriture lorquienne," *Bulletin Hispanique* 112:1 (June 2010): 373-395.

Calvo Serraller, Francisco. *La invención del arte español. De El Greco a Picasso*. Barcelona: Galaxia Gutenberg, 2013.

Cassin, Barbara and Emily S. Apter, editors. *Dictionary of Untranslatables: A Philosophical Lexicon*, Princeton University Press, 2014, s.v. "Duende."

Collin de Plancy, Jacques. *Diccionario infernal*. Vol. II. Barcelona, 1842. (Internet Archive)

Dobos, Erzsébet. *Conversaciones en La Habana. El episodio cubano de Federico García Lorca*. Budapest. Privately printed, 2008.

Eisenberg, Daniel. *Textos y documentos lorquianos*. Tallahassee, FLA. Privately printed, 1975.

Epstein, Jean. *La poésie d'aujourd'hui. Un nouvel état d'intelligence*, 2nd edition. Paris: Éditions de la Sirène, 1921.

Feliu, Daniel. *García Lorca, el duende en Rosario*. Rosario, Argentina: Baltasara Editora, 2016.

García, Carlos. *Federico García Lorca / Guillermo de Torre: Correspondencia y amistad*. Frankfurt Am Main: Vervuert, 2009

García, Miguel. *Queering Lorca's Duende: Desire, Death, Intermediality*. Cambridge: Legenda, 2022.

García Lorca, Federico. *Deep Song and Other Prose*. Edited and Translated by Christopher Maurer. New York: New Directions, 1980.

García Lorca, Federico. *Collected Poems*. Edited by Christopher Maurer. New York: Farrar, Straus and Giroux, 2002.

___. *Epistolario completo*. Ed. Andrew A. Anderson and Christopher Maurer. Madrid: Cátedra, 1998.

___. *Obras completas*, Edited by Miguel García-Posada. Barcelona: Galaxia Gutenberg / Círculo de Lectores, 1996-97.

___. *Palabra de Lorca. Declaraciones y entrevistas completas*. Edited by Victor Fernández and Rafael Inglada. Barcelona: Malpaso, 2017.

___. *Poet in New York*. Edited with an introduction by C. Maurer. Translated by Greg Simon and Steven F. White. Third edition. New York: Farrar, Straus and Giroux, 2013.

___. *Sun and Shadow*. Translated by R.M. Nadal and Kathleen Raine. London: Enitharmon Press, 1972.

García Lorca, Francisco. *In the Green Morning: Memories of Federico*. Translated by Christopher Maurer. New York: New Directions, 1986.

Gibson, Ian. *Federico García Lorca. 2. De Nueva York a Fuente Grande (1929-1936)*. Barcelona: Grijalbo, 1987.

Hernández, Mario. *Libro de los dibujos de Federico García*. Lorca Madrid: Tabapress/Fundación Federico García Lorca, 1990.

Hirsch, Edward. *The Demon and the Angel*. Boston: Houghton-Mifflin, 2002.

Iturria Savón, Miguel. *Miradas cubanas sobre García Lorca*. Sevilla: Renacimiento, 2006.

Juan de la Cruz. *Vida y obras*. Edited by Crisógono de Jesús, Matías del Niño Jesús and Lucinio Ruano. 6th ed. Madrid: Biblioteca de Autores Cristianos, 1972.

Laffranque, Marie. *Les idées esthétiques de Federico García Lorca*. Paris: Centre de Recherches Hispaniques, 1967.

Larrea Rubio, Pedro. *Federico García Lorca en Buenos Aires*. Seville: Renacimiento, 2015.

Lautréamont, Comte de. *Maldoror and the Complete Works*. Translated by Alexis Lykiard. Cambridge, MA: Exact Change, 1994. Internet Library.

León, José Javier. *El duende, hallazgo y cliché*. Prologue by Christopher Maurer. Seville: Athenaica, 2018.

___. "Flamenquísima, enduendada y torera. Santa Teresa, herida de amor," in *Jardín deshecho: Lorca y el amor*. Granada: Centro Federico García Lorca, 2019: 108-129.

___. *El pase de la muerte, de Ignacio Sánchez Mejías*. Seville: Athenaica, 2020.

___. *La sangre derramada. Ecos de la tauromaquia de Sánchez Mejías en García Lorca*. Prologue by Carlos Marzal. Seville: Athenaica, 2020.

Llano, Rafael. *La imagen-duende. García Lorca y Val del Omar*. Valencia: Pretextos/Fundación Gerardo Diego, 2014.

Lucretius. *De Rerum Natura / On the Nature of Things*. Translated by W.H.D. Rouse. Revised by Martin F. Smith. Cambridge, MA: Harvard University Press, 1992.

Ly, Nadine. "Lorca y la teoría de la escritura: 'La imagen poética de don Luis de Góngora,' in *Valoración actual de la obra de García Lorca: actas del coloquio celebrado en la Casa de Velázquez*. Edited by Alfonso Esteban and Jean-Pierre Étienvre. Madrid: Casa de Velázquez, 1988: 163-180.

Martínez Carmenate, Urbano. *García Lorca y Cuba: todas las aguas*. Havana: Centro de Investigación y Desarrollo de la Cultura Cubana Juan Marinello, 2002.

Martínez Torner, Eduardo. *Cancionero musical de la lírica popular asturiana*. Madrid: Nieto y Compañía, 1920. HathiTrust.

Maurer, Christopher, "Introducción," in Federico García Lorca, *Conferencias*, vol. I, Madrid: Alianza Editorial, 1984: 9-42.

____, editor. *Jardín deshecho. Lorca y el amor*. Granada: Centro Federico García Lorca, 2019.

Mayhew, Jonathan. *Apocryphal Lorca. Translation, Parody, Kitsch*. Chicago: University of Chicago Press, 2009.

____. "What Lorca Knew. A Reading of the Duende Lecture," in J.M., *Lorca's Legacy. Essays in Interpretation*. New York: Taylor & Francis Group, 2018.

Medina, Pablo. *Lorca. Un andaluz en Buenos Aires 1933-1934*. Buenos Aires: Manrique Zago / León Goldstein Editores, 1999.

Menéndez Pidal, Ramón. *Romancero hispánico (hispano-portugués, americano y sefardí) Teoría e historia*. Vol. 1. Madrid: Espasa-Calpe, 1953.

Monegal, Antonio. "Shall the Circle Be Unbroken? Verbal and Visual Poetry in Lorca, Buñuel y Dalí." *Bucknell Review* 45:1 (2001): 148-158.

Morla Lynch, Carlos. *Diarios epsañoles, Vol. I, 1928-1936*. Seville: Renacimiento, 2019.

Muñoz, Óscar Enrique. *La queja enamorada. Sobre el juego del duende de Federico García Lorca*. 3rd edition. Madrid: Mandala, 2013.

Nandorfy, Martha J. "Duende and Apocalypse in Lorca's Theory and Poetics." *Revista Canadiense de Estudios* 26:1/2 (2001): 255-270.

Nava, Alejandro. *In Search of Soul: Hip-Hop, Literature and Religion*. University of California Press, 2017.

Nietzsche, Friedrich. *Correspondencia*, vol. V. Madrid: Trotta, 2011.

Noonan, Philip. "From Stage to Page: Toward a History of the Literary Lecture in Spain (1900-1926)." PhD dissertation, Boston University, 2021.

Novo, Salvador. *Toda la prosa*. Mexico City: Empresas Editoriales, 1964.

Quance, Roberta. "On the Way to 'Duende' (Through Lorca's 'Elogio de

Antonia Mercé, la Argentina,' 1930)." *Tesserae: Journal of Iberian and Latin American Studies* 2-3 (2011): 181-94 .

Raeburn, Michael, editor. *Salvador Dalí: The Early Years*. London: South Bank Centre, 1994.

Rimbaud, Arthur. *Complete Works*. Translated by Paul Schmidt. New York: Harper Perennial, 2000.

Rodríguez Fernández, Javier. "Bound Hand and Foot: Lorca, Dalí and the 'Flight' of Surrealism." *Forum for Modern Language Studies* 58:1 (2022): 91-105.

Sánchez Mejías, Ignacio. "La tauromaquia," in *Sentimiento del toreo*, edited by C. Marzal, Barcelona: Tusquets, 2010: 115-127.

Silver, Philip. *La casa de Anteo. Ensayos de poética hispana (De Antonio Machado a Claudio Rodríguez)*. Translated by Salustiano Masó. Madrid: Taurus, 1985.

Soria Olmedo, Andrés. *Fábula de fuentes. Tradición y vida literaria en Federico García Lorca*. Madrid: Publicaciones de la Residencia de Estudiantes, 2004.

___. "Introducción," in Federico García Lorca, *Obras completas*, vol. I (*Prosa y poesía*). Madrid: Biblioteca Castro / Fundación José Antonio de Castro, 2019: xxxvii-cxxx.

Suárez Solis, Rafael. "Entre paréntesis. La evasión". *Diario de la Marina* (Havana), March 11 1930: 24.

Torre, Guillermo de. *Literaturas europeas de vanguardia*. Madrid: Caro Raggio, 1925.

Walsh, William Thomas. *St. Teresa of Avila. A Biography*. Milwaukee WI: Bruce Publishing, 1943.

Swan Isle Press is a not-for-profit publisher of literature
in translation including fiction, nonfiction, and poetry.

For information on books of related interest
or for a catalog of Swan Isle Press titles:
www.swanislepress.com

Finding Duende
Book and cover design by Marianne Jankowski
Typeset in Adobe Jensen Pro